MW00605110

A Youth Textbook of Chinese American History
Volume I

美华史记

青少年读本(一)

编写：潘秋辰、骆 西、程 汉

翻译：Rebecca Kuang, William Tang, Allan Zhao

封面设计：周 宇

插图：韩 梅

审定：Allan Zhao、苏 欣、唐孝先、程 汉

主编及监制：苏 欣

美华史记：华裔族群的共同记忆

Copyright© 2019. All rights reserved (Squircle LLC)

联系：youthhistory@gmail.com   order online: squircle.site

捐款荣誉墙

捐款个人：

李长胜、苏 欣、李薇艳、杨晓梅、蔡庆生、Kunal Paralikar、吴建平、肖长和、郭 华、远 方、刘 杰

捐款组织：

Asian Pacific Islander American Public Affairs (APAPA-Austin, 亚太联盟)
80-20 Education Foundation (80-20 教育基金会)
National Council of Chinese Americans (NCCA, 美国华人全国委员会)

****

《美华史记·青少年读本》的文章根据《美华史记》原创文章改编。

原创作者

黄 倩、苏 欣、骆 西、唐孝先、水 文、崔东娟、焦 凡、张为华、周 洁、陈树荣

潘秋辰： 畅销书作家，笔名秋辰、辰子。发表有多篇报告文学，并出版十余本书；现居美国华盛顿，活跃于华文创作领域。

骆 西： 毕业于四川大学中文系。热爱中文写作，有多年媒体和对外汉语教学经验，一直致力于华人社区服务和青少年教育。曾翻译出版《紫色云雾中的华西》。现居宾州。

Rebecca Kuang is pursuing an MPhil in China Studies at the University of Cambridge on a Marshall Scholarship. She graduated from the Odyssey Writing Workshop in 2016 and attended the CSSF Novel Writing Workshop in 2017. Her first novel *The Poppy War* was published by HarperCollins in 2018.

Allan Zhao is currently studying Aerospace Engineering at the University of California, Los Angeles. He loves reading about history, science, and politics and cares about social and ecomonic issues.

唐孝先(William Tang)：亚利桑那华人历史协会副会长、美国笔会专业会员、海明威学会会员。外语系英语专业，在高校任教英美语言文学课程多年。1989年为亚利桑那州立大学英文系访问学者。1995年出任亚利桑那州第一所教简体字的中文学校首任校长。

在美国《世界日报》发表人文类文章五十多篇。童年回忆录《故里神游》、译著《海明威在古巴》、文史专辑《尚俭堂文集》相继出版。曾受聘为美国贝立兹(Berlitz)国际语言学校教授中文，美国陆军一对一教授高级中文，中、英文授课。

韩 梅：十二年媒体工作经验，任《江南都市报》、《都市消费报》、《江西商报》的美术设计总监和美术编辑。十年美术教育工作经验。曾为"南昌广播电台音乐之声"和雄宇钢构公司等多家企业设计徽标。创刊设计和制作《中国国旅江西分公司》第一期旅游杂志。获得全国、省、市各项技能比赛一等奖。为多家杂志的插画师。现居美国怀俄明洲的夏延。

目 录

序

这是一个世代移民的故事，有过去，有现在。如月之恒，如日之升。

我们，一批具有在美国学习、生活和工作，拥有双语阅读和写作能力的华裔草根知识分子隆重推出了宏大的记录美国华人历史的工程——《美华史记》。"两脚踏东西文化"的人生经验和对民主法治的信仰是我们集体写作的基础。经过两年的历史研究和整理，我们为青少年献上了一份最为厚重的礼物《美华史记·青少年读本》。

《美华史记》诞生于 2017 年 4 月 25 日中午 12 点 28 分。一个平凡的时刻竟带来了意想不到的惊喜。那个时候我刚刚发表了一篇文章，文章的题目是《我们怎样书写属于我们时代的美国华人历史？》。因着这篇文章我和黄倩成了微信好友。黄倩个性热情开朗，爱憎分明，第一次聊天就把我的文章大大地赞扬了一番。后来认识久了才知道，只要你做与美国华人历史有关的事情，她就不吝惜地用任何语言来赞美你。每当我为项目烦恼时，一想到她那一口标准好听的北京腔，心中的愁云就全消了。她是一个有造诣，有实力，有激情的美国华人历史的研究和传播者。黄倩对我文章的赞美令我备受鼓舞。于是乎，我拉上远方建立了三个人的微信朋友圈。

认识远方是在明尼苏达州的一个微信群。2016 年大选前的一个晚上，远方刚一说话，就遭到一大群政见不同者的语言炸弹围攻他，这时他就发出一个小男孩盘着腿笑的动画图。当时我就觉得这个小男孩的形象就是远方了。其实，远方本人看上去厚重老成，年纪轻轻就长出很多的白发。他中等个头，腰板笔直，头总是微微高昂，毫无掩饰他的自信。数月之后，2017 年 2 月 7 日，远方拉我进入了他和陈爱国建的"陈建生维权群"。

陈建生是福建籍退休餐馆老板，无辜被枪杀。远方和陈爱国挑头带领明尼苏达州华人为陈建生伸张正义。他们二人有很多性格共性，独立、竞争、攻击、勇敢和仗义。不同的是远方有灵魂深处的清高和傲骨，而陈爱国有与生俱来的宽厚和处事的智慧。我和葛枚不知不觉地成了维权群里的骨干分子。葛枚知性、聪明、高挑、漂亮。她拥有高贵自由的灵魂，侠情不输远方和陈爱国，并且关心同胞的疾苦。她有持久的意志力和处理各种关系的天份，这些特质足以征服一切。就这样，当陈建生维权案告一段落后，远方提出成立一个非营利组织——美华联盟，随时帮助华人同胞，陈爱国、葛枚、远方和我四个人就这样走到了一起。

我是远方倡议成立美华联盟的第一个坚定的支持者。记得我下班回家路上，开车停在 65 号并入 694 号高速的路口，与远方在电话里商量美华联盟组织结构的问题，远方认为我有执行和管理能力，我认为远方有远见和洞察力，我们为美华联盟的领导一职推来推去。最后终于等到 694 号高速放行的一瞬，我们达成协议，远方先领头，之后我接上，没有投票章程的一个草根组织——美华联盟(The Association of Chinese American for Social Justice, ACASJ)从此奔上了无法回头的高速路。

远方一直有个想法，就是从律师事务所收集生活在美国的华人的故事，发表成系列文章，记录下我们华人同胞遇到的各种问题，以及怎样积极争取权利、走出困境并超越自我。2017 年 4 月 23 日美华联盟四人开会讨论工作计划时，我提出要开展推进 K-12 美华历史教育项目。这样，整理美华历史的想法就慢慢地融合起来。我的文章"我们怎样书写属于我们时代的美国华人历史？"正是配合这个想法而写。

黄倩、远方和我在三人朋友圈当即约定启动写作项目。微信记载 2017 年 4 月 25 日中午 12:56 分，我将三人朋友圈群名改为"美华历史写作"。我们首次认真考虑写几篇关于美国华人历史的文章，构思一个宏大的《美华史记》项目是以后慢慢形成和明朗化的。

微信的世界消息传播很快，写作群一下子由 3 人增加到 30 余人。当时我坚持作者管理规范化，每个作者和美华联盟签约。远方一直反对我的提议，他认为这种不给报酬的志愿服务不要签合同，我们应该鼓励所有人参与。其实我至今都不确定是不是当初应该听远方的，可是那时我们僵持不下，以远方的话，我一贯骄横跋扈，最后他提议我问一下作者。

虽然我坚持签约这个管理模式，但是对能否推行下去没有任何信心。我的第一个调查问卷投给了陈树荣。中午电话打过去，"我想和每个作者签合同，你觉得是否可以？"气量不足的沙哑南方口音传来，"当然要签！"他的态度坚决！这是第一次接触陈树荣。从此我们开启了坚固的友谊之旅。我们不常联系，只要联系就是有事相求，而我们有求就必应，从未让彼此失望过！

正是陈树荣的态度，我才将合同一一送了出去。然而，除了陈树荣外，没有任何阻力就签字送回的只有张华林和陈念洪。远方和我两人开始一一解释为什么要求大家签合同。我们的努力在前几个星期收效甚微。偏偏这时黄倩患病，寄给我一大纸盒子美华历史书。

她的数十本书似乎告诉我，"你们干吧，我不能参与了"。在黄倩治病期间，原来热闹的作者群所剩无几。

就这样，远方和我开始了艰难的招募作者工作，一切从零开始了。陈树荣讲过，"只要有三个作者，我们就能撑住美华历史写作系列。"我们咬紧牙关，闷头干活，看不到未来。

邀请唐梦加入写作项目时，就觉得她是北京电影学院的艺术系高才生，一直从事中美文化交流，是个不可多得的文科专业人才，没想她给我们带来了更大的惊喜。加入数周后，她就说，"我介绍你们认识我的先生王昶。"王昶律师毕业于北京电影学院，主修电影编剧及电影文学，是四个司法辖权律师。盛夏的八月六日，我们在明尼苏达州最大的商场(Mall of America) 的书店里见了面。闹中取静，正如浮华世界中的《美华史记》。我内心有些紧张，因为我们太需要一个撑得起写作项目的主编，王昶无疑是最佳人选。远方和我很经意地赴约。唐梦和我从没见过面，书店里她一眼就认出了我，而且坚持说我就是她微信中想象的样子。会晤持续了一个多小时。当下，王昶爽快地答应了我们的邀请，走马上任担当第一届《美华史记》的主编。

草根项目没有任何资金支持。联盟的组织注册费是群友李薇艳帮我们交的。第一笔$400 经费是陈爱国、葛枚、远方和我四人凑的。陈爱国开餐馆，每天工作 12 个小时，一周七天。我们开会就约到晚上 11 点。他们三人到我家开会时给我的第一笔现金带着体温。写作需要阅读大量文献和书籍。我们甚至没有资金购买参考书。以热衷公益事业而远近闻名的"马拉松花旗参"创始人姜铭涛博士慷慨地以首家赞助商身份提供帮助，支持我们的写作项目。慢慢地，我们的作者团队一点点壮大起来，黄倩病愈归队。终于万事俱备，《美华史记》系列文章终于在 2017 年 8 月 31 日星期四正式推出。

后来主编换届，我们有幸请到美国明尼苏达大学德卢斯校区的历史系教授方强接任。据远方说，他请方强到他的陋室吃了他做的便餐，他们就达成了君子约定。方强担任了很多业余职务--华东政法大学客座教授、美国中国历史学家学会(Chinese Historians in the United States)主席、荷兰阿姆斯特丹大学出版社"China in the New Era(新时代的中国)"主编和中文学校教师。他学术成就突出，发表了多部专著。他对《美华史记》文章的审稿和修稿的认真到了苛刻的程度。《美华史记》文章的质量在他的审阅下也随之提高，广受称赞。

志愿服务是一项想象不到的体力和精力的付出。《美华史记》作者们的劳动难以数量化。两年来我们发表了 60 多篇原创文章。这些作者们一路风雨，相扶相携，不言放弃。《美华史记》的作者是华人移民的代表，自尊，自强，自信，自立。

蝴蝶幼虫在生命发生质变的过程中，蛹要竭尽全力经过狭窄的蚕洞，小蚕洞帮助蛹长出翅翼，成蝶后才能振翅高飞。《美华史记》的成长和华人移民的过程恰似蝴蝶破茧，在痛苦中得到升华，拥有了飞翔的能力和力量。

让我们与《美华史记》相约，跟随文章一同前往沉睡的往昔岁月，朗读刻在我们心底的文字。

这是一个世代移民的故事，有过去，有将来。如山之寿，如松柏之茂盛。

这是一片神奇的土地，不似天涯，卷起杨花似雪花。

苏欣，写于美国明尼苏达州

2019 年 2 月 8 日

前 言

欢迎你，那些疲乏了的和贫困的，挤在一起渴望自由呼吸的大众，那熙熙攘攘的被遗弃了的、可怜的人们。把这些无家可归的、饱受颠沛的人们一起交给我。我站在金门，高举起自由的灯火！

犹太女诗人爱玛·拉扎露丝：《新巨人》
镌刻于自由女神像底座

《美华史记·青少年读本》立足于表现中华文化的源远流长和对美国华人历史的传承。本书有中文和英文相对照的两种语言，适用对象为会说双语的青少年，特别适用于学习中文的学生。文章有难度标识，可供水平不等的学生选择阅读。此书结合美国华人历史教育和中文的语言文化学习，使学生既能了解历史又能提高语言水平。考虑到美国本土青少年中文考试的实际需要，作者在文章中刻意加强了针对 AP、SAT 和 IB 测试的词汇、短语、语法、写作等训练，编写了对话、电邮、信函、便条、故事、诗歌、短剧等类型的文章和练习，可供学生尝试以多种形式锻炼语言表达技巧。

穿过百年历史长河，华人在美国留下了独特的印记：

➢ 1785 年四名受雇佣的中国水手乘"帕拉斯号"将亚洲货物运输到马里兰州巴尔的摩港；

➢ 1848 年至 1855 年淘金热时期，华人大量涌入加利福尼亚州；

➢ 1863 年美国动工修建太平洋铁路，中国劳工立下了汗马功劳；

➢ 1868 年美国政府与清政府签订的《中美天津条约续增条约》(即"蒲安臣条约")，美中两国民众可以自由到对方国家旅行以及长期居住；

➢ 1882 年美国总统切斯特·艾伦·阿瑟签署《关于执行有关华人条约诸规定的法律》(即"排华法案")；

➢ ……

➢ 1943 年"排华法案"被废止，允许每年 105 名华人移民入境；

➢ 2012 年美国国会通过正式决议，为曾经针对华人的歧视性法律道歉。

美国华人依靠自己的智慧、策略和韧性求生存，依靠勤奋、努力以及坚韧不拔的品质为美国社会的农业、法律、科学、经济等各行各业做出了巨大的贡献。由铁路建设到参军作战，时代赋予了华人前所未有的机遇和挑战。新一代和老一代移民，上一代和下一代移民，华人和美国社会不可分割。代代华人做着种种努力，书写了属于这个优秀族裔的家谱——美国华人历史。

苏欣
2018 年 12 月 22 日

 **The Association of Chinese Americans for Social Justice**

A Youth Textbook of Chinese American History
Volume I

美华史记
青少年读本(一)

编写：潘秋辰、骆 西、程 汉

翻译：Rebecca Kuang, William Tang, Allan Zhao

封面设计：周 宇

插图：韩 梅

审定：Allan Zhao、苏 欣、唐孝先、程 汉

主编及监制：苏 欣

美华史记：华裔族群的共同记忆

Copyright© 2019. All rights reserved (Squircle LLC)

联系：youthhistory@gmail.com   order online: squircle.site

145年后的荣誉

——纪念修建太平洋铁路的华裔先驱

骆 西

1869年5月10日，太平洋铁路的东段和西段在犹他州普洛芒特略山顶(Promontory Summit)汇合，整个工程宣告完工。2014年5月9日，美国劳工部将修建美国太平洋铁路的12000名华工载入劳工部名人堂①。在这之间，145年的时间已经过去了。劳工部名人堂设立于1988年。这也是第一次有亚裔美国人获得这一荣誉。重要的是，这项荣誉没有给予某个人，而是给予了一个群体。②

1850年代，美国还是个年轻的国家，从东到西的陆地交通极其不便。为了解决这一问题，急需修建一条连通东西的大铁路。太平洋铁路工程由联合太平洋铁路公司(Union Pacific)和中央太平洋铁路公司(Central Pacific Railroad)共同修建。于1863年开始，1869年完成。这项工程难度巨大，穿过了整个内华达山脉，全长3000多公里，被称为"自工业革命以来世界七大工业奇迹之一"。③太平洋铁路通车以后，使纽约到旧金山的行程从6个月缩短到了7天。俗话说，"要致富，先修路"。④大铁路为美国经济发展做出了巨大贡献。自此，美国也像乘上了高速列车，不断进步，并最终成为全世界最强大的国家。

太平洋铁路路线图连接爱荷华州的康瑟尔布拉夫斯、内布拉斯加州的奥马哈至加州旧金山湾东岸的奥克兰。Diagram of the transcontinental lines of road showing the original Central Pacific and Union Pacific and their competitors (1887). The report to the Congress of the United States, Senate Executive Document No. 51, 50th Congress, 1st Session, United States Pacific Railway Commission, digital image reconstruction and restoration by Centpacrr. The Cooper Collection of US Railroad History (CC-BY-SA, 1.0, 2.0, 2.5, 3.0).

在太平洋铁路的工程中，最困难的是内华达山脉段的建设。那么，是怎样的一群人完成了这 1100 公里铁轨的铺设？是谁在内华达的沙漠，雪花纷飞的群山间修建了 50 座桥梁，挖通了 10 多条山体隧道？为什么在历史里却找不到他们的名字？他们从哪里来，又到哪里去了？

从 1865 年到 1869 年间，约有 12000 名华工参与了大铁路的修建。他们是廉价的劳工，大多数来自中国的广东。在中央太平洋铁路公司雇佣的工人中，华工占百分之九十。虽然他们的平均身高只有 5 英尺，体重只有 100 磅，

但是却完成了超过常人两倍的工作。当其他工人在困难面前望而却步时，
华工们勇敢地接受了挑战。在 征 服合恩角(Cape Horn)的花岗岩和断壁
时，华工们的工具只有铁锤、凿子和 绳 子。他们不得不悬挂在半空中
安装火药。这项工作危险无比，很多华工因此丧命。在《美洲华侨史话》
中记载："在修建 100 英里的塞拉山脉(Sierra Crest)地段的铁路时，华
工的死亡率高达 10%以上。"华工们用杰出的表现证明了他们的工作能
力。虽然他们是廉价的劳动力，却也是了不起的建造者。

华工在合恩角的悬崖上工作。绘画来自 Mian Situ。At Cape Horn, the Chinese workers carved a roadbed around the steep peninsula high above the American River Canyon. Courtesy of Mian Situ.

华工们除了能吃苦耐劳，也是懂得运用智慧的能工巧匠（zhì huì néng gōng qiǎo jiàng）。1867 年冬天，气温降到摄氏零下 23 度(-23℃)，工程运输不得不中断。正在所有的工程师束手无策（shù shǒu wú cè）时，华工们用水制造了一条 59.5 公里的冰道。他们的点子不仅恢复了运输，还加快了工程的进度。这样的例子，在大铁路的建设中数不胜数（shù bú shèng shǔ）。

华工们不光是社会最底层的劳工，也是争取合法权利的斗士。⑤当时白人工人不光每月可以获得 35 美元的工资，铁路公司还提供食宿和人身保险。为了取得和白人工人相同的待遇，让工资从每月 26 美元提高到 35 美元，工作时间缩短到每天 8 小时，上千华工组织起来向铁路公司抗议。罢工持续了一周，期间他们的食品供应被切断。虽然最后华工的合理要求没有得到满足，但是他们为权利进行的斗争已经代表了一种觉醒。⑥

中央太平洋铁路在内华达的建造，上百名华工正在工作。Trestle on Central Pacific Railroad (1877). Photo by Carleton Watkins (1829-1916), Getty Center.

华工们为太平洋铁路的修建做出了巨大的贡献，有些甚至付出了生命的代价(成百上千的华工在爆破、山洞垮塌、泥石流、雪暴中丧生⑦)。可是在大铁路完工后，另一场为了尊严、平等的斗争才刚刚开始。近百年来，早期华人移民都不得不面对长期的种族歧视。特别是，1882 年由美国国会两院批准的《关于执行有关华人条约诸规定的法律》 (即"排华法案")将所有华人拒之门外；让已经在美国生活的华人永远无法取得合法身份成为美国公民。中国女性被禁止进入美国。这使在美国生活的华人男性要么无法与中国的妻儿团聚，要么很难在美国结婚，建立家庭。"排华法案"持续了 60 年，直到 1943 年才被废除。虽然太平洋铁路工程充分证明了华工的能力，可是他们仍然找不到工作。可以说，华裔社区在美国的建设是另一项艰巨的工程。

太平洋铁路完工后的合影，没有一个中国劳工在照片里。1869 年 5 月 10 日犹他州金钉庆祝仪式。在中间太平洋铁路公司 Samuel S. Montague（左中）与联合太平洋铁路公司(右中)的 Grenville M. Dodge 握手。The ceremony for the driving of the golden spike at Promontory Summit, Utah on May 10, 1869; completion of the First Transcontinental Railroad. At center left, Samuel S. Montague, Central Pacific Railroad, shakes hands with Grenville M. Dodge, Union Pacific Railroad，center right. Photo by Andrew J. Russell (1830-1902), National Archives and Records Administration, cataloged under the National Archives Identifier (NAID) 594940. ©

在今天，对于 400 万华裔美国人来说，为修建太平洋铁路而移民美国的华工是打开新大陆大门的先驱。⑧145 年来，他们的贡献被忘记，他们的故事不被诉说，现在他们终于获得了应有的荣誉。那些被埋葬（mái zàng）在铁路沿线无名的华工们也终于可以安息了。应该说，华工们的勇气、勤奋、忠于职责和自我牺牲的精神，不光帮助建造了太平洋铁路，也帮助建造了美国的民族精神。⑨他们在陌生（mò shēng）的国家，险恶的自然面前，没有被任何困难击倒，完成了"不可能完成"的任务。⑩虽然作为个人可能会死亡，可是作为一个群体他们坚持到了最后。太平洋铁路工程是华人留在美国历史中光辉的一页。新一代的华裔美国人仍然可以从先驱的精神遗产（jīngshén yí chǎn）中获得力量，为建设更美好的华裔社区，更美好的美国不断前行！

修建太平洋铁路的华工后裔与各地华裔齐聚犹他庆祝太平洋铁路建成通车。The descendants of Chinese workers who built the Pacific Railway from all over the world gathered to celebrate the anniversary of the completion of the Pacific Railway. Photo courtesy of National Park Service (Independence National Historical Park).

一、注解 Notes

① 2014 年 5 月 9 日，美国劳工部将修建美国太平洋铁路的 12000 名华工载入劳工部名人堂。

On 9 May 2014, the U.S. Department of Labor inducted the 12,000 Chinese laborers who had worked on the railroad into its Hall of Honor.

② 重要的是，这项荣誉没有给予某个人，而是给予了一个群体。

Significantly, this honor was not granted to any specific individual, but rather was granted to a group.

③ 这项工程难度巨大，穿过了整个内华达山脉，全长 3000 多公里，被称为"自工业革命以来世界七大工业奇迹之一"。

This engineering project faced extreme difficulties–it went through the entire Sierra Nevada mountain range, spanned 3000 kilometers in length, and was called the "one of the seven great industrial wonders of the world since the Industrial Revolution."

④ 俗话说，"要致富，先修路"。

It is said that "to get rich, first build roads."

⑤ 华工们不光是社会最底层的劳工，也是争取合法权利的斗士。

The Chinese laborers were not just workers at the lowest level of society; they were also fighters struggling for legal rights.

⑥ 虽然最后华工的合理要求没有得到满足，但是他们为权利进行的斗争已经代表了一种觉醒。

In the end, the Chinese workers' reasonable demands were not satisfied. However, their struggle for their rights represented a kind of awakening.

⑦ 成百上千的华工在爆破、山洞垮塌、泥石流、雪暴中丧生。

Hundreds of Chinese workers were killed in explosions, collapsed caves, landslides, and snowstorms.

⑧ 在今天，对于 400 万华裔美国人来说，为修建太平洋铁路而移民美国的华工是打开新大陆大门的先驱。

Today, to the four million Chinese Americans living in the US, the Chinese workers who immigrated to the United States to build the Pacific Railroad were pioneers who opened the doors to the New World.

⑨ 应该说，华工们的勇气、勤奋、忠于职责和自我牺牲的精神，不光帮助建造了太平洋铁路，也帮助建造了美国的民族精神。

It ought to be said that the Chinese workers' bravery, diligence, loyalty, responsibility, and spirit of self-sacrifice not only helped to build the Pacific Railroad, but also helped to build America's national spirit.

⑩ 他们在陌生的国家，险恶的自然面前，没有被任何困难击倒，完成了"不可能完成"的任务"。

In a strange land, facing the dangers of nature, they refused to be knocked down by difficulties and completed the task that could not be completed.

二、生词 New Words

荣誉	róng yù	honor
纪念	jì niàn	to commemorate
华工	huá gōng	Chinese worker
太平洋铁路	tài píng yáng tiě lù	Pacific Railroad
华裔	huá yì	Chinese descent
先驱	xiān qū	pioneer
劳工部	láo gōng bù	the Labor Department
名人堂	míng rén táng	Hall of Fame
载入	zǎi rù	to record
设立	shè lì	to set up/ to establish
陆地交通	lù dì jiāo tōng	land transportation
铺设	pū shè	to lay (铺设铁路-to lay railway)
山体隧道	shān tǐ suì dào	mountain tunnel
劳工	láo gōng	labor
廉价	lián jià	cheap , (廉价劳动力-cheap labor)
望而却步	wàng ér què bù	to shrink back at the sight of (something dangerous or difficult)
死亡率	sǐ wáng lù	mortality rate
吃苦耐劳	chī kǔ nài láo	to be inured to hardships
能工巧匠	néng gōng qiǎo jiàng	skilled craftsman
束手无策	shù shǒu wú cè	at one's wit's end
恢复	huī fù	to resume
数不胜数	shǔ bù shèng shǔ	countless

抗议	kàng yì	to protest
罢工	bà gōng	to strike
尊严	zūn yán	dignity
平等	píng děng	equality
排华法案	pái huá fǎ àn	the Chinese Exclusion Act
种族歧视	zhǒng zú qí shì	racial discrimination
拒之门外	jù zhī mén wài	to shut out
废除	fèi chú	to abolish
埋葬	mái zàng	to bury
安息	ān xī	to rest in peace
新一代	xīn yì dài	new generation
光辉	guāng huī	brilliant (光辉历史/光辉形象)
精神遗产	jīng shén yí chǎn	spiritual legacy

三、练习与运用 **Drills and Practice**：请注意文中有以下字词的句子，并用该字词造一个句子。

（一）在……中

在太平洋铁路的工程中，最困难的是内华达山脉段的建设。

<u>在学习中</u>，遇见困难是正常的。(学习)

_____，几乎看不见绿色植物。(沙漠)

_____，他的个子是最高的。(孩子)

（二）为了

为了解决这一问题，急需修建一条连通东西的大铁路。

_____, 他复习到很晚。(考试)

_____, 大卫决定到中国留学。(学习中文)

汉语插入语 Chinese interjections:

重要的是(The important thing is….)

俗话说(It is said….; As the saying goes….)

特别是(Especially)

可以说(It can be said….)

应该说(It ought to be said)

四、延伸思考 Extension Thinking

海明威说"人不是生来就是被打败的。你可以尽可能的去消灭他，但就是打不败他。"在《145 年后的荣誉》一文中，为什么说"虽然作为个人可能会死亡，可是作为一个群体他们坚持到了最后"？

Hemingway said, "But man is not made for defeat. A man can be destroyed but not defeated." In *A Glory 145 Years Late: Remembering the Chinese Pioneers Who Built the Pacific Railroad*, what do we mean by "as individuals they may have died, but as a group they persevered to the end"?

A Glory 145 Years Late: Remembering the Chinese Pioneers Who Built the Pacific Railroad

Translated by Rebecca Kuang

On 10 May 1869, when the eastern and western segments of the Pacific Railroad met at Promontory Summit, Utah, the entire project was declared finished. On 9 May 2014, the U.S. Department of Labor inducted 12,000 Chinese laborers who had worked on the railroad into its Hall of Honor. By that time, 145 years had already passed. The U.S. Department of Labor Hall of Honor was created in 1998. This was the first time that Asian Americans had been granted this honor. Significantly, this honor was not granted to any specific individual, but rather was granted to a group.

In the 1850s, America was still a young country, and travelling by land from east to west was extremely difficult. In order to resolve this problem, a long railroad to connect its eastern and western coasts was urgently needed. The Union Pacific and Central Pacific railroad companies collaborated on the Pacific Railroad construction project, which was begun in 1863 and finished in 1869. This engineering project faced extreme difficulties–it went through the entire Sierra Nevada mountain range, spanned 3000 kilometers in length, and was called the "one of the seven great industrial wonders of the world since the Industrial Revolution." After the Pacific Railroad opened, the journey from New York to San Francisco was shortened from six months to seven days. It is said that "to get rich, first build roads." The great railroad greatly contributed to America's economic growth. Since then, the United States has seemed to be riding a high-speed train, constantly progressing, and finally becoming the world's most powerful country.

During the construction of the Pacific Railroad, the most difficult stretch was in the Sierra Nevada. How did a group of people finish laying the tracks for this 1100 kilometer stretch of the railroad? Who constructed fifty bridges and dug more than ten tunnels through stone among the snowy mountains and deserts of Nevada? Why can't we find their names in the historical record? Where did they come from, and where did they go?

From 1865 to 1869, about 12,000 Chinese workers participated in the construction of the Great Railroad. They were cheap labor, and most of them were from China's Guangdong province. Among the laborers hired by the Central Pacific Railroad Company, the Chinese comprised ninety percent. Even though their average height was only five feet and their average weight one hundred pounds, they completed twice as much work as the average person. While other workers flinched in the face of hardship, Chinese workers bravely welcomed challenges. When conquering the granite cliffs and craggy walls of Cape Horn, the Chinese workers had only iron hammers, chisels, and rope. They had no choice but to install gunpowder while hanging in midair. This work was dangerous beyond compare, and many Chinese laborers lost their lives. In "A History of the Overseas Chinese in America", it is recorded that "while building the hundred-mile railroad segment in the Sierra Crest, the death rate of Chinese workers was higher than ten percent." The Chinese laborers' outstanding performance proved their competence. They may have been a cheap labor force, but they were excellent construction workers.

Apart from being diligent and able to endure hardships, the Chinese laborers were skilled and clever workmen. In the winter of 1867, the temperature fell past minus 23 degrees Celsius (-23°C), forcing transportation to the construction zone to cease. While all the engineers were at loss for what to do, the Chinese laborers used water to manufacture a 59.5-kilometer long path made of ice. This idea not only restored transportation, but it also increased the pace of the project. During the construction of the great railroad, cases like this are too many to count.

The Chinese laborers were not just workers at the lowest level of society, they were also fighters struggling for legal rights. At the time, white laborers earned thirty-five dollars salary every month; in addition, the railroad company provided them with room, board, and life insurance.

Over a thousand Chinese workers organized to protest against the railroad companies in order to obtain the same treatment as white workers: a salary increase from twenty-six to thirty-five dollars per month and shortened working hours to eight hours each day. They went on strike for a week, during which time their food provisions were cut off. In the end, the Chinese workers' reasonable demands were not satisfied. However, their struggle for their rights represented a kind of awakening.

Chinese laborers greatly contributed to the construction of the Pacific Railroad. Some even sacrificed their lives (hundreds of Chinese workers were killed in explosions, collapsed caves, landslides, and snowstorms). However, when the great railroad was completed, another struggle for dignity and equality had just begun. Over the past century, the early Chinese immigrants faced a long period of racial discrimination. In particular, in 1882, the two chambers of Congress ratified the Chinese Exclusion Act (An Act to Execute Certain Treaty Stipulations Relating to the

Chinese) and closed America's doors to all Chinese people. This left Chinese people already living in America without any way to ever obtain legal status as American citizens. Chinese women were prohibited from entering the United States. This meant Chinese men living in the United States had no way to reunite with their wives or children. It also made it difficult for them to get married or establish a household in the United States. The Chinese Exclusion Act remained in effect for sixty years and was only abolished in 1943. The Pacific Railroad construction project had amply demonstrated the capabilities of Chinese workers, but they were still unable to find work. It can be said that the construction of Chinese communities in America was a difficult project of its own.

Today, to the four million Chinese Americans living in the US, the Chinese workers who immigrated to the United States to build the Pacific Railroad were pioneers who opened the doors to the New World. A hundred and forty-five years later, their contributions had been forgotten, and their stories had not been told. Now, they have finally gained their proper glory. Those nameless Chinese laborers who are buried along the railroad tracks can finally rest in peace. It ought to be said that the Chinese workers' bravery, diligence, loyalty, responsibility, and spirit of self-sacrifice not only helped to build the Pacific Railroad, but also helped to build America's national spirit. In a strange land, facing the dangers of nature, they refused to be knocked down by difficulties and completed the task that could not be completed. As individuals they may have died, but as a group they persevered to the end. The Pacific Railroad project is a glorious chapter in the history of the Chinese in the United States. To the new generation of Chinese Americans, we can still draw strength from the legacy of our forebears' spirit and advance unceasingly to construct a better Chinese community and a better America.

华工在八号东隧道口。Chinese railroad worker. "Heading of east portal Tunnel No. 8" by Alfred Hart (1865-1869). Courtesy of the Library of Congress. ⌀

一堂生动的历史课

——第一位到美国的中国小伙

改编：骆 西
原创：黄 倩

人物：李大伟、爸爸、妈妈、黄老师

李大伟(David)今年 16 岁，出生在美国，他非常喜欢历史。夏天父母带他去波士顿玩。波士顿建于 1630 年，是美国最古老的城市之一。这里既有著名的哈佛大学(建于 1636 年)，也有波士顿公共图书馆。波士顿公共图书馆是仅次于美国国会图书馆和纽约公共图书馆的美国第三大公共图书馆。可是父母的好友黄倩老师并没有带他们去参观这些地方，而是为他们安排了一次特别的活动——寻访第一位到美国的中国小伙。通过阅读这个故事，同学们可以发现历史并不只在书本里，历史也在我们的身边。特别是美国华人的故事，还有很多需要同学们自己去发现、整理和书写。俗话说"世上无难事，只怕有心人"。①来吧，同学们去找一找家里的老照片；去跟祖父母聊一聊；到自己生活的城市里去问一问，说不定你也可以成为美国华人历史的发现者。

(一) 波士顿中央公园

李大伟： 波士顿中央公园太有意思了，真不愧是美国最古老的城市公园。

黄老师： 大伟，你的中文说得真好！平时你都是怎么学习的？

李大伟：黄老师，谢谢您的夸奖。我每个周末都去中文学校。平时在家，妈妈也会帮助我学习中文。

黄老师：除了学中文，你还喜欢些什么？

李大伟：我还喜欢看书，特别是跟历史有关的书。所以这次能来波士顿旅游，我特别兴奋。

黄老师：哦，那太好了！

李大伟：黄老师，还要走多久才能见到我们要去访问的人呢？

黄老师：你看，我们就快到了。

妈妈：黄老师，你确定我们要见的人就住在这里？前面就是中央公园的中央墓地了(Central Burying Ground)。

黄老师：是的，我们要访问的人就住在里面。他算得上是第一位到美国的中国小伙，已经在这里长眠了 220 年了。②

爸爸：真没想到在波士顿公园的中央墓地里居然还埋葬了一位中国人。

黄老师：是的，很多中国人也都不知道。这也是为什么我要带你们来这里看看的原因。

妈妈：他的墓地在哪里呢？

黄老师：我们一起来找找吧。

妈妈：这是美国最早的诗人父子斯布拉格(Samuel and Charles Sprague)的墓碑。

李大伟：这是美国肖像画家斯图尔特(Gilbert Stuart)的墓碑，他还为华盛顿总统画过肖 像 (portrait)呢！

爸爸：我找到了，你们快过来看看。

在此地长眠的是一位姓周(Chow)的中国人，终年 19 岁。1798 年 9 月 11 日，他从波士顿"麦克"号船只的桅杆(mast)上坠落致死。他的主人在此立碑，以示深切缅怀(to pay respects)。

——约翰·小博伊特(John Boit Jr.)

破译信息 decoding needed:

1. The information above is most likely translated from

A. An advertisement.

B. A tombstone.

C. A missing person poster.

D. A love letter.

2. Which of the following statements is TRUE?

A. Here is a person who is sleeping.

B. Here is a person who fell from a carriage.

C. This tombstone was placed by John Boit Jr. for Zhou (Chow).

D. This tombstone was placed by Zhou for John Boit Jr.

****

《美华史记》项目组联系到波士顿公园管理局，建议在周的墓地设立标识、添加历史人物介绍。波士顿公园管理局告知，将于 2019 年完成这项工作。

周的墓。黄倩拍摄。A tombstone of Zhou (Chow). Photo by Qian Huang.

李大伟：这位姓周的中国人是怎么来美国的呢？美国独立之前，英国人一直控制着美国和其他国家之间的茶叶贸易，所以才有了 1773 年发生的波士顿倾茶事件和之后 1775 年发生的早期殖民者反抗大英帝国(British Empire) 统治的独立战争。1783 年推翻了英国统治，成为一个独立国家。我也读到过中美贸易的历史。1784 年第一艘美国商船从纽约出发到达了中国广东的黄埔港。这条船的名字叫"中国皇后"号。这个时期的中美贸易从 1783 年算起，一直到 1844 年，持续了半个多世纪，为美国制造了一大批百万富翁，也被称为"老中国贸易 (Old China Trade)"。难道这位姓周的"小伙子"就是坐着美国的商船来的？

黄老师：大伟，你的历史知识真丰富。波士顿是美国最早与广东进行贸易的地方，也是当时最重要的港口之一。从中国返回的美国商船需要带上一些当地的中国人在船上干活。这位姓周的小伙子肯定不是船上唯一的中国人。但是因为他在波士顿港口不幸身亡，他的墓地又被好好的保存到了现在，可以说他的墓地是迄今为止在美国发现的最早的华人墓地。这说明中国人在美国的历史远比已有历史记载的更久。除此，我还在 1798 年<u>波士顿政府死亡人口档案</u>(Deaths registered in the city of Boston)中找到了这位中国小伙的名字。

李大伟：黄老师，真佩服您有这样的发现。

黄老师：大伟，历史不光在书本里，历史也在我们的身边。只要用心，我们每个人都可以做美国华人历史的发现者。

3. When did the first American merchant ship arrive in Guangdong, China?

      A. 1773   B. 1783

      C. 1775   D. 1784

4. How did this young fellow come to the United States?

      A. 坐飞机   B. 坐火车

      C. 坐船   D. 坐汽车

5. Why is the discovery of Zhou's graveyard important for the history of Chinese Americans?

A. His graveyard has been well preserved.

B. His graveyard has a history of 220 years.

C. The name on the tombstone matches government documents.

D. All of the above.

(二) 谁是约翰·小博伊特？

在找到了姓周的中国小伙的墓地之后，李大伟又对墓碑上的美国人约翰·小博伊特(John Boit Jr.)产生了兴趣。黄老师将小博伊特的《环球航海日志》拿给大伟阅读。

约翰·小博伊特是周(Chow)的老板。小博伊特的父亲是波士顿的进口(import trade)商人。小博伊特的姐夫(brother-in-law)有一艘远洋帆船。小博伊特16岁就开始跟着姐夫进行环球航行。19岁时，他就可以独自远航了。他最著名的事件是和姐夫一起在华盛顿地区发现了一条河流。因为他们的船叫"哥伦比亚"号，所以那条河也被取名为"哥伦比亚"河。之后，小博伊特在哥伦比亚河捕捉水獭(otter)，将水獭皮卖到中国，再从中国进口茶叶与丝绸卖到美国。小博伊特是最早从事中美贸易的先驱(pioneer)。

小博伊特曾两次进行环球航行。第一次航行时，小博伊特才16岁。在船上他负责写航海日志。第二次航行时，小博伊特19岁。两次航行，他都到达了中国广东。在第二次航行时，小博伊特将周带来了美国。周在1796年离开中国广东，他当时的年龄是17岁。

在小博伊特的的家史(family history)中，小博伊特称周为"我忠实的仆人"。这也是为什么在周不幸去世后，小博伊特为他修建了很好的墓地，让他可以在异国他乡的土地上安息。

6. How old was John Boit Jr. when he started sailing globally?

    A. 19   B. 17

    C. 16   D. 15

7. Which of the following statements is FALSE?

A. John Boit Jr. sold otter furs to China.

B. John Boit Jr. and his father discovered and named the Columbia River.

C. John Boit Jr. liked Zhou.

D. John Boit Jr. was responsible for writing a journal about the voyage.

注解 NOTE：

① 俗话说"世上无难事，只怕有心人"。

As the saying goes, no task is impossible as long as one has a determined heart.

② 他算得上是第一位到美国的中国小伙，已经在这里长眠了 220 年了。 长眠 is a euphemism for death.

收藏于波士顿艺术馆约翰·小博伊特的后代画像。图片中可以看见中国花瓶。The Daughters of Edward Darley Boit. Painting by John Singer Sargent (1882). Museum of Fine Arts, Boston.

Reference：
美华史记|最早来到美国的中国小伙
https://mp.weixin.qq.com/s/RZ2AaBlDp7XlPKMHvclLpQ

A Lively History Lesson: Investigating the First Chinese Man to Come to America

Translated by Rebecca Kuang

Characters: David Li, Father, Mother, and Teacher Huang

David Li is sixteen years old. He was born in the United States, and he really likes history. His parents have brought him to Boston for his summer vacation. Boston was founded in 1630, making it one of America's oldest cities. Boston has Harvard University (founded in 1636), as well as the Boston Public Library. The Boston Public library is the third-largest public library in the United States behind only the Library of Congress and the New York Public Library. However, Teacher Qian Huang, a good friend of David's parents, has not taken them to see these sights, but has arranged a unique activity instead: finding the first Chinese man to come to the United States. By reading through this story, students will discover that history is not just on the page, but exists all around us. There remain many stories of Chinese American history for students to discover, organize, and write about. As the saying goes, no task is impossible as long as one has a determined heart. Come, students. Go look at your old family photos. Talk to your grandparents. Go ask around the city that you live in. Perhaps you can also discover new things in the history of Chinese Americans.

1. Boston Common

David: Boston Common is so fascinating. It's the oldest city park in the United States.

Teacher Huang: David, your Chinese is so good! How do you usually study?

David: Teacher Huang, thank you for your compliment. I go to Chinese School every weekend. My mother also regularly helps me practice my Chinese at home.

Teacher Huang: What else do you like to do aside from studying Chinese?

David: I also enjoy reading. I especially like books about history. That's why I'm so excited about this trip to Boston.

Teacher Huang: That's fantastic!

David: Teacher Huang, how long do we have to go until we meet the man we're going to visit?

Teacher Huang: Look, we're almost there.

Mother: Teacher Huang, are you sure the person we're meeting is here? The Central Burying Ground is right in front of us.

Teacher Huang: Yes, the man we are visiting is right here. He is the first Chinese person to come to the United States. He has slept here for 220 years.

Father: Who would have imagined that a Chinese person would be buried in the Central Burying Ground?

Teacher Huang: Yes, many Chinese people don't know about this. That's the reason why I brought you here.

Mother: Where is his grave?

Teacher Huang: Let's look together.

Mother: Here are the graves of one of America's first poets, Samuel Sprague and his father Charles Sprague.

David: Here's the tombstone of the portraitist Gilbert Stuart. He painted Washington's portrait.

Father: I found it. Quickly, come look!

Taken from gravestone: Here lies interred the body of Chow Manderien, a native of China, aged 19 years, whose death was occasioned on the 11th of Sept 1798 by a fall from the masthead of the ship Mac of Boston. This stone erected to his memory by his affectionate master John Boit Jr.

David: How did this Chinese person by the name of Zhou (Chow) come to the United States? Before America's independence, England controlled the tea trade between America and other countries. This was the cause of the Boston Tea Party in 1773. Afterwards, the American Revolution for independence from the British Empire began in 1775. The residents of Great Britain's North American colonies overthrew British rule in 1783 and became an independent nation. I've also read about the history of US-China relations. In 1784, the first American merchant ship to reach China left from New York to Guangdong. This ship was called the *Empress of China*. This period of trade, also known as the "Old China Trade", lasted over half a century between 1784 to 1844 and created many wealthy men in the United States. Could it be that this fellow named Zhou came here on an American merchant trip?

Teacher Huang: David, you certainly have a good understanding of history! Boston was the first American city to initiate trade with Guangdong. It was also one of the most important ports at the time. American ships returning from China needed to bring along some local Chinese workers. This fellow named Zhou was certainly not the only Chinese person on that ship. But because he unfortunately died in Boston, his grave has been well preserved until today. So far, his grave is the oldest grave found of a Chinese person in the United States. This shows that the history of the Chinese in America goes far back beyond what the historical record suggests. I found this fellow's name in the public records of deaths registered in the city of Boston.

 David: Teacher Huang, I greatly admire you for your discovery.

 Teacher Huang: David, history is not just in textbooks. History is all around us. If we just pay attention, all of us can discover new things in Chinese American history.

2. Who is John Boit Jr.?

After he found the grave of the fellow named Zhou, David became interested in the grave of an American man named John Boit Jr. Teacher Huang gave Boit's diaries of a voyage around the world to David to read.

John Boit Jr. was Chow's (Zhou's) boss. John's father was a businessman working in the import trade in Boston. John Boit Jr.'s brother-in-law owned a trading vessel. At the age of sixteen, John Boit Jr. began to sail around the world with his brother-in-law. He was sailing long distances on his own by the time he was nineteen. He is most famous for discovering a river in the Washington area with his brother-in-law. Because their ship was called the Colombia, the river was also named the Columbia River. Later, little John Boit Jr. sold the otter furs trapped by the Columbia River to China and imported tea and silk from China to the United States. John Boit Jr. was one of the first pioneers of the Sino-American trade.

John Boit Jr. sailed around the world twice. On his first voyage, he was only sixteen years old. His duties onboard included writing in the ship logbook. On his second voyage, he was nineteen years old. On both trips, he arrived in Guangdong. It was on this second voyage that John Boit Jr. brought Zhou to the United States. When Zhou left Guangdong in 1796, he was only seventeen years old.

In the Boit family records, John Boit Jr. called Zhou "my loyal servant." This is reason why, after Zhou's unfortunate death, John Boit Jr. ensured he was buried with a good tombstone so that he could rest peacefully in a foreign land.

中国城天使

改编：潘秋辰
原创：唐孝先

十九世纪中叶，加利福尼亚地区发现了金矿，大约有 30 万人从美国其他地区和国外涌入加利福尼亚。中国淘金矿工进入美国的第一站便是旧金山。于是，从 1850 年开始，旧金山的中国社区渐趋形成，今天，也被称为中国城(华埠^{huá bù})。

旧金山中国城。Chinatown, San Francisco (ca.1895). Photo by Wilhelm Hester. Wilhelm Hester Photographs Collection, University of Washington.

1874 年，旧金山唐人街 920 号(920 Sacramento Street, San Francisco, CA 94108)，建起了一幢五层楼高的红砖建筑，这里是唐人街基督教长老会传道院的所在地(Presbyterian Mission House)。

那么，这所传道院与华人又有什么不解的渊源呢？

淘金时代，美国西部妇女奇缺，卖淫在美国西部很多民族中相当普遍。华人移民社区的卖淫业是旧金山的严重问题。1875 年 3 月 3 日美国立法系统通过《佩奇法案》禁止所谓的廉价劳动力及"不道德"的亚裔妇女进入美国。《佩奇法案》加剧了美国华人男女比例失衡，反常地鼓励了它声称要打击的罪行：卖淫。很多贫苦家庭，受封建社会重男轻女思想影响，很容易听信人贩子的花言巧语，真的以为美国遍地黄金，女儿交由他们带去是享福。当时，人口贩子将大量中国东南沿海的妇女带入美国。这种买卖人口的现象被称为"黄奴贸易(The Yellow Slave Trade)"。

这些华人妹仔(Mui Tsais)到达美国后，被华人黑社会帮派以曾替她们支付从中国来美国的一大笔旅费为由，把她们卖到富人家做婢女，或卖入妓院做妓女。

清光绪十二年(1886 年)，一位名叫"新金"的华女，签了一份卖身契：自愿将身为妓，价钱 1205 美元，合约四年半，银不计利，人不计工，患病送返中国，如怀孕则合约延长一年。至今，这份用毛笔书写的卖身契还陈列在唐人街基督教长老会传道院内。

那些卖到富人家伺候主子的女孩，深受凌辱[líng rǔ]、家暴，很多女孩常常活不过五年就因不堪折磨而死。因此，很多不堪忍受的华人女孩冒死逃出来寻求社会救助，而且人数越来越多。

旧金山市政当局知道人口买卖的事，但没有任何行动。中华总会馆(俗称六大公司)想出来干涉，然而面对强大的黑帮势力，也无能为力。

唐纳蒂娜·卡梅伦。A portrait of Donaldina Cameron as a young woman (1922). Photo from gravesite.com.

这时候，有一位白人女性出现了，她的名字是唐纳蒂娜·卡梅伦(Donaldina Cameron)，1869 年 7 月 26 日出生在一个苏格兰家庭，是家里七个孩子中最小的一个。1871 年，她随家人搬到了加利福尼亚州的圣华金河谷(San Joaquin Valley)。她自幼在富人圈子里长大，并未接触过移民。

有一次，父母的朋友玛丽·布朗(Mary P.D. Browne)女士带小卡梅伦来到长老会传道院，她第一次看到一些亚洲姑娘获得救助后聚集在这里，看书识字，学习英文，做缝纫活[féng rèn]等等，井然有序[jǐng rán yǒu xù]地组成了一个纯女性的小社会。这件事给小卡梅伦留下了深刻的印象。

31

1895 年，她在长老会传道院的支持下，和玛格丽特·卡尔伯森 (Margaret Culbertson)一起，在旧金山妇女外宣传道委员会下属的长老会传道院开始救助华人妇女。1900 年，卡梅隆接任了长老会传道院院长职务。她被华人女孩悲惨(bēi cǎn)的命运所震惊(zhènjīng)，她利用自己是白人，又属于基督教会的有利条件，把长老会传道院改成了"华人妇女之家"，成为华人妇女的庇护所(bì hù suǒ)。她还给自己起了个中文名字"金美伦"。救助回来的姑娘亲切地称呼她"老母 (Lo Mo) "，而仇恨她的人口贩子、帮派分子则称她"番鬼(fān guǐ)(Fahn Quai)"。

华人妇女庇护所经常遭受人口贩子骚扰(sāo rǎo)，卡梅伦除了求助于警察和教会，还在庇护所内开了一条秘密通道，人口贩子有时突然闯进这里找逃跑的妇女，金美伦就让她们从通道逃离。

卡梅伦的正义行动很快在中国城产生了强烈反响，不断有华人女孩前来寻求救助。也有人半夜递纸条密报，说哪里囚禁(qiú jìn)了华人女孩，哪个姑娘身陷淫窝等，她听说后立即前往搜救。

卡梅伦和孩子们。Cameron and children (1907). Courtesy of the Presbyterian Historical Society.

卡梅伦生就一副硬朗的面孔，正气凛然(zhèng qì lǐn rán)，嫉恶如仇(jí è rú chóu)，一般人都很敬畏(jìng wèi)她。英文报纸上称她为"中国城愤怒的天使(the Angry Angel of Chinatown)"。因她对华人妇女的遭遇愤愤不平(fèn fèn bù píng)，对那些把妇女同胞当作货物买卖赚钱(zhuànqián)，剥夺她们尊严(zūn yán)和人权的恶势力(è shì lì)愤恨至极。因此，这位不同凡响的女士在华埠有一个响当当的称呼——中国城天使。

从 1895 年到 1934 年退休的三十九年间，卡梅伦营救了约 3000 名沦为奴婢、妓女的华人妇女。被营救出来的华人女子，住在长老会传道院内，不能单独外出，外出须有人陪同。院方向她们传教，教她们习读《圣经》，慢慢使她们接受并信仰基督教。当时从国内贩卖来的华人女孩很少上学读书，传道院就帮她们制定了严格的英文学习课程，还教习她们学会西方家庭主妇操持的各种家务、家政、缝纫、生活技能等，经过相当一段时间的教习后，为她们择基督徒男子为夫，女孩就此离开传道院，建立起自己的家庭，过上了自己的生活，有了一个安稳的家。

OCCIDENTAL BOARD HEADQUARTERS AND MISSION HOME, 920 Sacramento St., San Francisco.

地震毁坏的长老会传道院(左)和金美伦堂(右)。The Mission Home after earthquake (left, 1906. Courtesy of the Presbyterian Historical Society ⓒ) and Cameron House (right, 2018. Photo by mliu92, CC-BY-SA, 2.0).

长老会传道院（华人女子庇护所）在1906年地震引发的火灾中被烧毁，后又重建。1942年，正式更名为金美伦堂(Cameron House)，以此纪念这位唐人街天使的伟大善举。

1968年1月4日，卡梅伦在旧金山附近的帕洛阿尔托(Palo Alto)去世，享年98岁，终生未婚。

练习

一、生词 **New Words**：将以下词语注上拼音。

华埠	Chinatown	_____	
婢女	maid	_____	
凌辱	to insult	_____	
庇护所	shelter	_____	

伺候 to serve _____

缝纫 sewing _____

囚禁 in captivity _____

骚扰 harassment _____

卖身契 a contract to sell oneself _____

重男轻女 to treat woman as inferior to men _____

人口贩子 traffickers _____

花言巧语 rhetoric, to coax with luring words _____

无能为力 powerless, unable to do anything _____

井然有序 orderly _____

正义凛然 righteously _____

愤愤不平 aggrieved, indignant _____

嫉恶如仇 to hate evil as one's enemy _____

不同凡响 outstanding _____

二、有趣的动物成语，请在括号内填上一种动物。**Please put an animal in the brackets to create an interesting animal idioms.**

一（　　）当先　　　　引（　　）入室　　　　放（　　）归山

一箭双（　　）　　　　打草惊（　　）　　　　画（　　）点睛

（　　）到成功　　　　（　　）语花香　　　　如（　　）添翼

（　　）不停蹄　　　　群（　　）无首　　　　如（　　）得水

快（　　）加鞭　　　　对（　　）弹琴　　　　（　　）飞（　　）舞

（　　）毛蒜皮　　　　（　　）飞蛋打　　　　生（　　）活（　　）

画（　　）添足　　　　（　　）口余生　　　　（　　）争（　　）斗

盲人摸（　　）　　　　爱屋及（　　）　　　　（　　）吞（　　）咽

胆小如（　　）　　　　骑（　　）难下

前怕（　　），后怕（　　）

路遥知（　　）力，日久见人心

三、**Drills and Practice**：请注意文中有以下字词的句子，并用该字词造一个句子。

(一) 虽然……但是……还是……

虽然买卖人口是不合法的，但是黑帮组织为了赚钱，还是将中国东南沿海的女性骗到美国卖为奴婢或妓女。

_____

(二) 虽然……可是……

当年，长老会传道院虽然救助了很多人华人女子，可是依然没有彻底杜绝买卖华人妇女的现象。

35

(三) 虽然......不过......却......;

虽然华人单身女性不能进入美国，不过狡猾的人口贩子却以假结婚的方式，把她们骗到美国来。

(四) 尽管......但是......;

华人在美国尽管辛苦做工，但是没有尊严和地位。

(五) 尽管......可是......;

尽管卡梅伦女士已经救助了约 3000 名华人女性，可是已经有很多女性死在异国他乡了。

(六) 尽管......不过......却......;

尽管被骗到美国来的华人女性从来没有读过书，不过在传道院里，却学到了许多文化知识和生活技能。

(七) 然而......却......;

然而这些华人女性在嫁给基督徒丈夫后，却过上了安稳的生活，摆脱了悲惨的命运。

(八) 由于......因此......;

由于在旧金山金矿做劳工的华人男性多，女性少，因此造成了男女比例严重失调，男性想成家非常难。

36

(九) 由于......因而......;

由于卡梅伦像天使一样保护了很多受害的中国女性，因而她被称为唐人街天使。

(十) 因为......，所以......;

因为卡梅伦女士把救助所有受害妇女当作自己的使命，所以她无暇顾及自己的婚姻大事，终生未嫁。

四、判断正误，请在正确的句子前面写"T"，错误的句子前面写"F"
Please write "T" before correct sentences and "F" before incorrect sentences：

( ) 1. Ms. Cameron helped Chinese women because she was of Chinese descent.

( ) 2. Traffickers brought Chinese women to the United States and sold them, with their consent, to wealthy families or brothels.

( ) 3. Chinatowns are found in every city in America. They are streets where Chinese goods are sold.

( ) 4. Donaldina received the title "the angry angel of Chinatown" because she was angry at all the actions taken against women.

( ) 5. Cameron spent her life rescuing more than 3000 Chinese women and raising shelters so they could live a happy life.

五、请从文中出现的下列成语中，选三个成语写一段话。

花言巧语、嫉恶如仇、井然有序、无能为力、不同凡响、正义凛然

_____

_____

_____

_____

_____

_____

_____

_____

_____

_____

_____

_____

References：

1. 美华史记｜旧金山唐人街上的天使
https://mp.weixin.qq.com/s/ro1OMNBAL2Ec_Ewyw94Gyg
2. 美华史记｜十九世纪的女性华人及佩奇法案
https://mp.weixin.qq.com/s/hqJhen0QCK8iSwXoGiMejg
3. Chinatown's Angry Angel: The Story of Donaldina Cameron by Mildred Crowl Martin.
Pacific Book Pub.

Chinatown's Angel

Translated by William Tang

In the mid-19th century, gold mines were discovered in California. Approximately 300,000 people flooded into California from the rest of the United States and abroad. The first stop for Chinese gold miners to enter the United States was San Francisco. As a result, from 1850, the Chinese communities of San Francisco gradually came into being. Today, it is called Chinatown.

In 1874, a five-story red-brick building was built up at 920 Sacramento Street, San Francisco, CA 94108, which was the Presbyterian Mission House in Chinatown.

So what was the relationship between this Presbyterian Mission House and the Chinese?

During the gold rush, women were scarce in the western United States, and prostitution was common among many ethnic groups in the west. Prostitution in Chinese immigrant communities was a serious problem in San Francisco. On March 3, 1875, the U.S. legislative system passed the Page Act, which prohibited the entry of so-called cheap labor and "immoral" Asian women to the United States. The Page Act exacerbated the gender imbalance among Chinese Americans, perversely encouraging the crime it claimed to fight: prostitution. Many poor families, influenced by the feudal society's preference for sons over daughters, were easily persuaded by the rhetoric of human traffickers. They really believed that there was gold everywhere in the United States and that their daughters would be taken by them to enjoy happiness. At that time, human traffickers brought large number of women from southeast coasts of China into the United States. The demographic phenomenon was known as the "the Yellow Slave Trade".

In the 12th year of the reign of Emperor Guangxu of the Qing Dynasty (1886), a Chinese woman named "Xin Jin" signed a contract of prostitution: she volunteered to be a prostitute for the price of $1,205. The contract was effective for four and a half years. The paid money would not gain interest, and the hours would be unlimited. If she were sick, she would be sent back to China. If she were pregnant, the contract would be extended by one year. The deed of sale, written with a brush, is still on display at the Presbyterian Mission House in Chinatown.

The girls who were sold to rich families to serve their masters were subjected to abuse and domestic violence, and many girls were tortured to death within the first five years. Therefore, many desperate Chinese girls risked their lives to escape and seek social assistance, and the number was increasing.

San Francisco City Hall knew about the trafficking but did nothing about it. The Chinese Consolidated Benevolent Association (commonly known as the Chinese Six Companies) wanted to intervene, but in the face of powerful gangsters, there was nothing they could do.

Just then, a white woman appeared. Her name was Donaldina Cameron. She was born on July 26, 1869, into a Scottish family, the youngest of the seven children. In 1871, her family moved to the San Joaquin Valley of California. She was brought up in a circle of wealthy families, and she had very little contact and experience with immigration population.

Once, Mary P.D. Browne, a friend of her parents, took young Cameron to the Presbyterian Home. She saw some Asian girls gathered here after they were rescued for the first time. The girls learned how to read and write, learned English, housekeeping skills and so on. They appeared to form a genuine female society. This event made a deep impression on young Cameron.

In 1895, Donaldina began to work with Chinese women, joining Margaret Culbertson, under the auspices of the Presbyterian Church, at the mission home of the Woman's Occidental Board of Foreign Missions in San Francisco. In 1900, Cameron became superintendent of the home. She was shocked by the tragic fate of the Chinese girls. She took advantage of her being a white woman and a member of a Christian church to change the Presbyterian Home into a "Chinese women's home", and it became a place of refuge for Chinese women. She even gave herself a Chinese name "Jin Meilun". The rescued girls affectionately called her "Lo Mo" while the human traffickers and gang members who hated her called her "Fahn Quai".

The Chinese women's shelter was often harassed by traffickers. Cameron, in addition to seeking help from the police and the church, had dug a secret tunnel in the shelter. Sometimes the traffickers would suddenly break in to look for fleeing women. Cameron would let the girls escape through the tunnel.

Cameron's justice actions quickly reverberated in Chinatown. Chinese girls sought help continuously. In addition, people would pass notes in the middle of the night, saying where Chinese women were imprisoned and which girl was caught in a brothel, and she would immediately go to search and rescue.

Cameron was born with strong convictions, hated injustice like poison, and average people were in awe of her. The English newspapers called her "Chinatown's angry angel" for her indignance towards those who bought and sold women. She deeply resented the evil forces that deprived her compatriots of their dignity and human rights. As a result, the defiant woman had a loud name in Chinatown—the Angel of Chinatown.

Between 1895 and 1934, she rescued about 3,000 Chinese women who had become slaves or prostitutes. The Chinese women who were rescued lived in the Presbyterian Mission House. They were not allowed to go out alone; others would accompany them. The missionaries preached to them, taught them to read the Bible, and slowly made them accept and believe in Christianity. At that time, almost none of the trafficked girls received any education. The mission developed strict English learning courses and taught them various kinds of housework, housekeeping, sewing and living skills of western housewives. After a considerable period, they could choose Christian men as their husbands. The girls left the Presbyterian Mission House and set up their own families. They lived their own lives and had steady homes.

The Presbyterian Mission House, at the same time the Chinese women's shelter, was burned in a fire caused by the 1906 earthquake. It was rebuilt. In 1942, it was officially renamed Cameron House, a tribute to the great kindness of Chinatown's angel.

On January 4, 1968, Donaldina Cameron passed away in Palo Alto, near San Francisco, when she was 98. She remained single all her life.

中国领事洋律师

——傅列秘传略

改编：程 汉

原创：黄 倩

1878 年 12 月 12 日，中国驻旧金山总领事馆开馆。在领馆人员中，有一位美国籍的领事傅列秘(Frederick Bee)。中国领事馆为什么会挑选一位美国人当领事呢？

这要从那个时代的历史讲起。

美国十九世纪七十年代开始的经济衰退，使得加州的当地欧洲移民都把矛头对准了在种族、肤色、语言、文化、宗教和生活习俗上与他们完全不同的华人，认为是这个群体抢夺了他们的工作机会，侵吞了他们的财富。于是，排华运动开始了。

排华者打出了"让中国人无立锥之地！"的口号，扬言要"武力解决"；"假如中国佬不肯走，我们就把他们送到海里"；"如果投票办不了，我们就用子弹解决！"他们运来枪支，计划焚烧华工的伐木场，用炸药摧毁唐人街。排华从言论升级为行动，向越来越多的区域蔓延。

在越来越恶劣的环境中，只有傅列秘等少数美国人挺身而出，为华人发
出了公道的呐喊。

nà hǎn

傅列秘原来是纽约的律师。1855 年他开始在加州经营矿业，是一位成功
的企业家。他开发了索萨利托市(Sausalito)，管理铁路建设，并在内华达山
脉上建了一个电报公司。

傅列秘像。Frederick Bee (1879 to 1888). Ralston Family Collection, Lewis & Clark College
Aubrey Watzek Library Archives and Special Collections.

他的企业雇佣过 20 名中国矿工。他们的勤劳与能干使得他印象深刻。加州的金矿区有很多华工，他们工作繁重^{fán zhòng}但是报酬^{bào chou}很少，更为不公的是社会地位极为低下。

每当看到华工受到不公正的对待时，傅列秘就会出手相助，帮助他们维护权益。在他被聘^{pìn}为三藩市中华会馆(六大公司)法律顾问期间，经常以律师身份为基于种族原因被指控犯罪的华人尽心辩护。1876 年，在没有一个律师愿意站在华人一边的情势下，傅列秘挺身而出^{tǐng shēn ér chū}担任了华人的律师，多次在国会的中国问题调查委员会作证，接受媒体采访。他的刚正、热情与能力，在华人中建立起极好的口碑^{kǒu bēi}。

傅列秘用自己的经历和事实表明了对中国人的看法：中国人"忠厚而诚实"，干活"没人能超过他们。他们辛勤地劳作，每一分钱工资都是挣来的"。"在南加州修路时要经过沙漠，那里烈日灼人^{liè rì zhuó rén}，无论给多少钱白人都不去；若不是中国人，那条路就永远也修不起来。"他驳斥了"华人只是干体力活或者做家庭仆人"的说法："完全不对。很多中国人是成功的生意人"，并以详细的海关数据证明了华人对于当地经济的贡献。他认为，加州优秀市民阶层眼中的中国人是良好市民。对于排华运动，他怒斥说：因为劳动力匮乏，"美国内战期间和修建铁路时我们都鼓励中国人来"，中国人没有抢白人饭碗。而现在反对中国人的，就是"几年前在纽约放火烧医院的那种人，还有七月暴乱时破坏哈里斯堡和匹兹堡火车站的那种人"！

中国首任驻美公使陈兰彬称赞傅列秘是凡遇华人有事，总是愿意出面想办法解决的"真心卫顾、始终不懈^{xiè}者"，还把他比作中国古代的大侠。公使觉

45

得交涉事件纷繁，需要熟悉情况的美国人帮助，而傅列秘在品质和能力上都是最合适的。就这样，他成了总领事馆的领事。

十九世纪八十年代，排华逆流愈演愈烈。担任了领事的傅列秘也面对着越来越复杂的局面和越来越繁重的任务。每有排华事件发生，傅列秘都立即行动，乘火车或是蒸汽船，甚至是骑马奔赴现场；他的现场调查和详实取证，成为中国对美国外交交涉的牢实基础。

1880 年的丹佛暴乱中，一名华人被打死，另一名华人被割去双耳。中国公使根据傅列秘的调查报告，向美国国务院提出了抗议照会。

这张图片记录了丹佛排华暴乱的野蛮与疯狂。The Anti-Chinese Riot in Denver on October 31. Frank Leslie´s Illustrated Newspaper (1880). Courtesy of the Museum of Chinese in America, New York, N.Y., USA. ⊘

1882 年 3 月，傅列秘在给激烈辩论《关于执行有关华人条约诸规定的法律》 (即"排华法案")的国会的信里警告："法案"违背了美国的立国之本；"我相信《独立宣言》的不朽真谛与'黄金定律'和'山上宝训'来自同一个源头"；"一百年前国父们无疑踏上了一条通向平安、强大与荣耀(róng yào)的道路，而我们现在要走的道路却恰恰通向耻辱(chǐ rǔ)，软弱与危险。"

1884 年，出生在美国的华人孩子梅蜜(Mamie)入读公立学校被拒。傅列秘立即向市教育局提出了抗议；他在给市、州学监公函(gōng hán)中指出：这种行为既违反了中美之间的现行条约，也违反了美国宪法和加州法律。最后，这件事得到了建立专门的华人学校的局部胜利。

1885 年 9 月，怀俄明州石泉镇的欧洲移民矿工因为不满华工不参加罢工而发动屠杀，造成四十余人伤亡。傅列秘代表中国提出诉讼索赔(sù sòng suǒ péi)，要求惩(chéng)处暴民(chǔ bào mín)与镇长。

1886 年，西雅图地区连续发生暴力驱逐(qū zhú)华人的事件。傅列秘请求地方政府和联邦政府干预；并致电州长警告说 "心地邪恶(xīn dì xié è)的家伙杀害了几个中国人，进一步的暴力将会随时爆发"。当年，他代表保护华人的少数派在国会发言，驳斥了排华分子污蔑(wū miè)华人的谎言："中国人的瑕疵(xiá cī)白人全都有，然而中国人勤劳、节俭、温和、平静、年底保证不欠债这些美德，白人却做不到几条。白人没有理由用华人和白人活法不一样作为借口而驱逐他们。"

1889 年，一个华人遭到税收官员殴打。傅列秘坚决要求逮捕(dài bǔ)那个打人的官员，并将此事向媒体公布。

傅列秘的主持正义自然引起排华者们的敌视。有报纸发表社论，公开指责傅列秘"不是个好美国人"；也有报纸刊登了丑化、侮辱他的漫画；他收到过要他"30 天之内离开加州，否则要你的命"的恐吓信；甚至有人公开集资要暗杀他。 但是，他从来没有退缩过。中国使节黄遵宪回忆，在一次协助华人入境时，一名白人持枪威胁说："敢帮助他们，叫你尝尝子弹！"傅列秘立即从靴子里拔出一把手枪，对着那人说："你敢？！"

1892 年 5 月 26 日，66 岁的傅列秘去世。在那个最黑暗、最冰冷的日子里，美国华人为他们的"老朋友"——这位华人维权战场上百折不挠的勇敢者下半旗致哀。今天的加利福尼亚州索萨利托市还有一条以他的名字命名的街道。

加利福尼亚州索萨利托市傅列秘街。The Bee Street. Photo courtesy of Anthony Oertel.

一、生词 New Words：请为文中下列词语标注上拼音。

立锥之地	_____	律师	_____
税收官员	_____	公使	_____
立锥之地	_____	律师	_____
税收官员	_____	公使	_____
挺身而出	_____	领事	_____
百折不挠	_____	火车	_____
驻外机构	_____	骑马	_____
总领事馆	_____	蒸汽船	_____
独立宣言	_____	美国籍	_____
经济衰退	_____	企业家	_____
美国宪法	_____	美国内战	_____
加州法律	_____	欧洲移民	_____

二、**Drills and Practice**：请注意文中有以下字词的句子，并用该字词造一个句子。

（一）呢？

中国领事馆为什么会挑选一位美国人当领事呢？

_____

（二）更、最

加州的金矿区有很多华工，他们工作繁重但是报酬很少，更为不公的是社会地位极为低下。(比较的用法)

傅列秘在品质和能力上都是最合适的。

在那个最黑暗、最冰冷的日子里，美国华人为他们的"老朋友"——这位华人维权战场上百折不挠的勇敢者下半旗致哀。

最后，这件事得到了建立专门的华人学校的局部胜利。

（三）越来越

排华从言论升级为行动，向越来越多的区域蔓延。

在越来越恶劣的环境中，只有傅列秘等少数美国人挺身而出，为华人发出了公道的呐喊。

担任了领事的傅列秘也面对着越来越复杂的局面和越来越繁重的任务。

（四）就

每当看到华工受到不公正的对待时，傅列秘就会出手相助，帮助他们维护权益。(表示时间上的及时)

现在反对中国人的，就是"几年前在纽约放火烧医院的那种人"。

(一种强调的用法)

就这样，他成了总领事馆的领事。(一种强调的用法)

(五) 将、把

傅列秘坚决要求逮捕那个打人的官员，并将此事向媒体公布。

加州的当地白人和欧洲移民都把矛头对准了在种族、肤色、语言、文化、宗教和生活习俗上与他们完全不同的华人。

中国首任驻美公使把傅列秘比作中国古代的大侠。

傅列秘立即从靴子里拔出一把手枪。(量词)

(六) 被

1880 年的丹佛暴乱中，一名华人被(一名白人)打死，另一名华人被(一名白人)割去双耳。(名词+被+名词+动词)

1884 年，出生在美国的华人孩子梅蜜(Mamie)入读公立学校被拒。(名词+被+动词)

（七）无论……，都……

在南加州修路时要经过沙漠，那里烈日灼人，无论给多少钱白人都不去。

（八）不是……，就……

若不是中国人，那条路就永远也修不起来。

（九）假如……就(就要、就能、就会/就可以)……

假如中国佬不肯走，我们就(能，会，可以)把他们送到海里。

（十）要是……就(就要、就能、就会/就可以)……

要是(如果)投票办不了，我们就(能，会，可以)用子弹解决。

三、在地图上找出下面几个州或城市

加利福尼亚州(加州)、怀俄明州、石泉镇、西雅图、旧金山(三藩市)、纽约、哈里斯堡、匹兹堡。

The National Map. Courtesy of the U.S. Geological Survey.

References:
1. 美华史记 | 洋律师出任光绪皇帝的外交官
http://mp.weixin.qq.com/s/iPhJ07DQCg_nggptUWLExg
2. 美华史记 | 石泉大屠杀始末：火海中的华工，百年的沉痛
https://mp.weixin.qq.com/s/stXy91qzYwl1cHWdTQ_WEg

A Brief Biography of Frederick Bee: The American Lawyer Who Became a Chinese Consul

Translated by Rebecca Kuang

On 12 December 1878, China opened a consulate in San Francisco. Among the consulate personnel was an American consul named Frederick Bee. Why would the Chinese consulate choose an American for this job?

We must start by discussing the history of that era.

In the 1870s, the United States was undergoing an economic recession. This caused European immigrants in California to target Chinese people, who differed from them in race, skin color, language, culture, religion, lifestyle, customs and traditions. They believed the Chinese had stolen both their wealth and job opportunities. An anti-Chinese movement began as a result.

The anti-Chinese camp began using the slogan "The Chinese Must Go!" (No Place for a Chinaman) and threatened a "forceful solution": "If the Chinese won't go, we'll have to send them into the ocean;" "If voting can't resolve this, we'll use bullets!" They brought guns and made plans to burn down the Chinese laborers' logging areas. They also planned to use explosives to destroy Chinatown. The anti-Chinese movement escalated from words to actions as it spread to more and more areas.

In this increasingly hostile environment, only Frederick Bee and a small number of Americans bravely stepped forward to demand justice for Chinese Americans.

Bee was originally a lawyer from New York. In 1855, he started a mining operation in California. He was quite a successful entrepreneur—he developed the City of Sausalito, managed railroad construction, and built a telegraph company over the Sierra Nevada Mountains.

His mining company employed twenty Chinese laborers. Their diligence and competence left a deep impression on Bee. There were many Chinese laborers working in the gold mines of California. However, they received very little reward for their hard labor. Even more unjust was their low social position.

Every time Bee saw a Chinese laborer receiving unfair treatment, he extended his hand to help protect their interest and rights. While he was serving as a legal advisor to the Chinese Consolidated Benevolent Association (the Chinese Six Companies) in San Francisco, he often advocated, to the best of his ability, as a lawyer on behalf of Chinese immigrants who had been accused of crimes based on racist principles. In

1876, a time when not a single lawyer would stand on the side of the Chinese, Bee stepped forward to be their lawyer. He testified often in front of the Congressional committee to investigate Chinese immigration and spoke out in media interviews. His honesty, passion, and competence won him an excellent reputation among the Chinese community.

Bee used both facts and his personal experience to clearly state his opinion on the Chinese: he argued that the Chinese were honest and truthful. No one was a better worker than the Chinese. They worked diligently, and they earned every penny of their wages. In California, road repair efforts required laborers to suffer the scorching heat of the sun in the desert. White laborers refused that work no matter how much money they were offered. Without the Chinese, that road would never have been built. He refuted the stereotype that the Chinese were only good for hard labor and household service jobs: "This is totally incorrect. Many Chinese people are successful businessmen." He also used customs data to prove that Chinese immigration benefited the local economy. He believed that in the eyes of California's citizens of good standing, the Chinese were excellent citizens.

He angrily rebuked the anti-Chinese movement: because of labor shortages, "during the American Civil War and the construction of the railroad, we encouraged Chinese people to come." Chinese people hadn't stolen white people's abilities to make a living. Moreover, the anti-Chinese demonstrators were "the type of people who set fire to a hospital in New York a few years ago, and the type of people destroyed train stations in Harrisburg and Pittsburgh in riots in July."

The first Chinese foreign minister to the United States, Chen Lanbin praised Bee for helping the Chinese find solutions whenever problems arose "with sincerity and persistence." He even compared Bee to a noble warrior from Chinese antiquity. The foreign minister believed that negotiations would be complicated, and that he therefore needed the help of an American who was familiar with the situation. Bee's personal character and experience made him well-suited for the job. Thus, Bee was appointed as a consul of the Chinese consulate.

In the 1880s, the anti-Chinese movement grew more and more intense. After becoming consul, Bee faced increasingly complicated situations and shouldered heavier and heavier duties. Every time an anti-Chinese incident took place, Bee immediately took action, hurrying to the scene by train, by steamboat, or even by horse. His on-site investigation and detailed, accurate evidence collection formed a solid basis for Chinese diplomatic negotiations with the United States.

During the Denver Riot of 1880, one Chinese man was killed and another Chinese man had his ears cut off. The Chinese foreign minister sent the American State Department a diplomatic note in protest based on Bee's investigative report.

In March of 1882, Bee sent a letter regarding the debate over the Chinese Exclusion Act (An Act to Execute Certain Treaty Stipulations Relating to the Chinese) to Congress, warning that this proposed bill violated the founding principles of the United States: "I believe that the immortal truths of the Declaration of Independence came from the same source with the Golden Rule and the Sermon on the Mount. As surely as the path on which our fathers entered a hundred years ago led to safety, to strength, to glory, so surely will the path on which we now propose to enter bring us to shame, to weakness, and to peril."

In 1884, Mamie Tape, a Chinese American child born in the United States, was refused entrance to the local public school. Bee immediately protested to the city education bureau. In a letter to the city and state superintendents, he wrote that this kind of action violated the current treaty in effect between China and the United States, as well as California state law and the American Constitution. In the end, this resulted in a partial victory for the construction of schools specifically for Chinese students.

In September 1885, European immigrants working as miners in Rock Springs, Wyoming attacked a group of Chinese laborers, who they resented for not joining them on a labor strike. Over forty people were killed or injured in the bloodbath. Bee represented the Chinese in a lawsuit to demand reparations and requested that both the rioters and the city mayor be punished.

In 1886, the Seattle region was hit by a series of violent expulsions of the Chinese. Bee requested both the state government and federal government to intervene. He also sent a telegram to the state governor warning that: "Wicked people have murdered several Chinese. Further violence could break out at any moment." That year, he made a speech, on behalf of the minority group protecting Chinese people, to Congress in which he refuted the lies that the anti-Chinese movement had created to slander the Chinese: "The flaws of the Chinese are ones possessed by Whites as well. However, Chinese people are hardworking, frugal, gentle, peaceful, and don't owe debts at the end of the year. These are virtues that some white people don't possess. Whites have no grounds to use the argument that the Chinese live differently from us as an excuse to expel them."

In 1889, a Chinese American was beaten by a tax official. Bee firmly requested that the official be arrested and made this incident known to the media.

Naturally, Bee's fight for justice won him the enmity of the anti-Chinese demonstrators. One newspaper published an editorial criticizing Bee for "not being a good American." Another newspaper published a cartoon that vilified and insulted him. Bee received a letter demanding that he "leave California within 30 days, or you're dead." Public funds were even raised for his assassination. But he never cowered. The Chinese diplomatic envoy Huang Zunxian recalled that one time when Bee was helping Chinese immigrants enter the United States, a white man threatened him with a gun and said that if Bee dared to help the Chinese, he would let him taste his bullets. Bee immediately pulled a pistol from his boot and asked the man if he dared.

On 26 May 1892, the 66-year-old Bee passed away. During those darkest, coldest days, the Chinese-American community flew their flags at half-mast to mourn their brave old friend who, despite all setbacks, had fought hard on the battlefield for their rights. Today, there is a street named after him in Sausalito, California.

看图写作训练

Photo 1 by James Reilly, J. J. Chung Collection. Photo 2 by Bain News Service, Library of Congress. Photos 3-6 by Miriam and Ira D. Wallach Division of Art. Photos 3 & 5 from Robert N. Dennis collection; Photo 4 from Stephen A. Schwarzman; Photo 6 from Detroit Publishing Company postcards. ⓔ

上面的图片是1880-1900年前后旧金山和纽约中国城的中餐馆内外的场景。写一篇关于中餐馆的过去和现在变迁的议论文体的文章(non-fiction)。

_____

_____

_____

_____

_____

_____

_____

_____

_____

_____

_____

_____

_____

加州工人党和"排华法案"

改编：潘秋辰

原创：苏 欣

清朝后期中国国力 guó lì shuāi jié 衰 竭，mín bù liáo shēng 民不聊 生 。西方列强制造了" huánghuò 黄 祸 (Yellow Peril) "一词，shāndòng 煽 动 人们对华人的 kǒng jù 恐 惧 与 chóuhèn 仇 恨 。

商品广告上卡通显示，山姆大叔要将华人踢出美国。The magic washer, manufactured by Geo. Dee, Dixon, Illinois. The Chinese must go, Chicago: Shober & Carqueville Lith Co., c1886. Library of Congress.

美国历史上，1873 至 1878 年正值全国经济大萧条时期，1877 年加州工

人党在失业大军中应运而生，次年便控制了加州立法机关，掌握了修立宪

法的权力。加州工人党中有一名劳工领袖，名叫丹尼斯·科尼，他认为华人

是"廉价的工作奴隶"，他们的劳动削弱了美国人的生活水准，应该从美国

淘汰出去，继而大肆利用种族主义观点排挤中国移民。

科尼(1847-1907)，爱尔兰裔美国政治领袖。Denis Kearney (1847-1907), Irish-American political leader, influential in the passing of the Chinese Exclusion Act of 1882. UC Berkeley, Bancroft Library. ⓔ

　　其实，在经济大萧条时期，雇主为降低成本，更愿意保留廉价的华工，

裁减白人从业者，于是，白人把失业的原因都归咎到中国人头上。

　　　　　fā　xiè yuàn qì
无法发泄怨气的民众很快被科尼公开的种族主义思潮所煽动，开始无
　　　　　　　　　　　　　　　　　　　　　　　　　　　　　　shāndòng

　　　xíngjìng　　　　　　　　　　　　　　　　bào fā　　zhènjīng　　　　　　sāoluàn
端支持种种反华行径，1877 年 7 月 23 日，爆发了震惊历史的旧金山骚乱，

以白人为主对中国移民进行了为期两天的大规模暴动。

讽刺漫画显示"一名异教徒"兴高采烈地讽刺关在旧金山监狱中的科尼。Elation of the "heathen Chinee" over a recent event in San Francisco. "Caricature of a Chinese man pointing and laughing at Denis Kearney in San Francisco jail" (1880). Courtesy of the Library of Congress.

　　这一天，加州工人党召开了一个特别会议，约 8000 人从四面八方涌入了
　　　　　　　　　　　　　　　　　　　　　dǎohuǒsuǒ
旧金山市政厅广场。工人党领袖把失业问题的导火索引向中国移民，引发了

　　　　　　　　　　　　　　jué le dī
失业大潮中这座火山的爆发，大批人像决了堤的河水一般涌入唐人街，疯狂

进行了两天打砸抢暴行。导致四名中国人死亡，20 家中国洗衣店被摧毁，损失超过 10 万美元。

7 月 24 日晚，在警察、州国民卫队和一千名社区公民自卫队共同努力下，种族暴动才被制止。科尼反倒因为帮助平息这场骚乱而成为崭露头角的人物，从此他开始推动美国的反华运动，直到促成 1882 年 5 月 6 日美国国会出台了历史上臭名昭著的《关于执行有关华人条约诸规定的法律》(即"排华法案")。

"排华法案"出台后，华人被打到了社会最底层，在美国尤其是西北部地区发生了大量针对华人的暴力攻击事件。但"排华法案"的诞生并不是一蹴而就的，早在通过该项法案的 30 多年前，就已经开始了针对华人的诸多不合理规定。

杂志上的一页显示着漫画评论"排华法案"，一名中国男子坐在自由金门之外，旁边的标语上写着"注意：我们欢迎共产主义、虚无主义、社会主义、芬安和流氓，但中国佬不能进入"。The only one barred out Enlightened American statesman - "We must draw the line somewhere, you know." Digital file from original, whole page，New York: Frank Leslie (1882). Courtesy of the Library of Congress. ✎

比如：1850 年加州征收外国矿工税，外国主要指中国矿工所在的矿区；

1852 年转向债券^{zhàiquàn}法案要求船长准备一份外国旅客名单，船东要求每个到达加州的人购买 500 美元的债券，这项资金可以转向用于每位乘客 5 至 50 美元的税收。当时正值加州淘金热，有 20026 名华工作为廉价劳动力来到这里从事辛苦的金矿淘金业，但外国矿工税从 3 美元上涨到 4 美元，许多矿区还禁止中国人开采；1854 年加州最高法院不允许中国人作证反对白人；1855 年通过了"限制不能成为公民的国家移民"议案。加州一些县，对无入籍资格的人其实就是中国人，征收 50 美元入籍税，还规定运载每个中国移民要征收 50 美元"人头税"。

还有 1858 年加州通过一项限制中国和蒙古人移民的"法案"；1860 年旧金山市医院不接受中国病人；加州北部的公立学校禁止接收中国儿童，并于 1866 年修订中改为在白人家长不反对的情况下，华裔儿童可以去白人学校上学；1862 年，第 37 届美国国会通过了"反苦力"法，禁止美国公民在美国船只上进行苦力交易；1870 年旧金山的市政工程项目禁止雇用中国人，城市禁止使用扁担挑菜；并允许移民官员随意判断中国妇女是否为妓女；要求中国男子出示品德良好证明才能入境；当年，"反苦力"法实施八年后允许非洲人通过归化成为公民，但是继续排除亚洲人，尤其是中国人。几十个州通过了禁止非公民购买房地产的外国土地法，中国移民不能投票^{tóu piào}和陪审^{péi shěn}，不能拥有土地，不能建立永久性住房和企业；1873 年旧金山规定洗衣店如用扁担^{biǎndan}运输衣服每季度收 15 美元，而用马车运输每季度交 2 美元；1873 年旧金山限制华人节庆时放鞭炮^{biānpào}、敲礼仪锣^{luó}；1875 年旧金山通过一个反辫子法律，不剪头发将被抓入监狱^{jiān yù}。旧金山还要求居室要有 500 立方英尺空间，杜绝中

国穷人挤在一个小的公寓里。1875年加州规定虾网大小，从而减少中国渔民

bǔ lāo liàng
捕捞量。

随后，1876 年立法规定联邦政府对移民法规有绝对权力；1879 年加州宪法禁止公司和市政工程雇用中国人，中国人被限定到城市边界外的特定地区；1880 年旧金山抗熨衣条例禁止洗衣的夜间操作。加州通过一个"钓鱼法"，禁止中国人从事钓鱼业务。1880 年通过修订 1868 年的《中美天津条约续增条约》(即"蒲安臣条约")，推出了《安吉立条约》，限制中国劳工入美；1882 年旧金山新洗衣许可法要求中国洗衣业要有许可证。加州立法机关声明反华示威允以公假。历史走到这一年，最终以"排华法案"正式通过生效而达到巅峰。

其实，在那个年代，中国人做的是白人不愿意做的苦工，比如淘砂、耕地、开洗衣店、开餐馆、做家佣等等。可是，一旦白人失业了，就觉得是中国人偷走了自己不屑于做的工作机会。他们自认为是"优势"种族，甚至以

fēngkuáng zī zhǎng
与中国人并肩工作为耻。在此期间，白人报复势头疯 狂 滋 长 起来，种族骚乱和冲突时有发生，1871 年，洛杉矶发生暴力侵害事件，有 17 至 20 名中国人在一夜之间被绞死。"排华法案"生效十二年后，美国国会又增加了新条款，更为直接地限制中国移民入籍。

在此后漫长的六十一年岁月中，美国华人生活在不平等、不民主的法律阴影中，直到 1943 年被废止，1965 年被彻底解除。

练 习

一、生词 New Words：请用英文说出文中下列词语的意思。

崭露	zhǎn loù	_____	暴动	bào dòng	_____
廉价	lián jià	_____	摧毁	cuī huǐ	_____
废止	fèi zhǐ	_____	萧条	xiāo tiáo	_____
不屑	bú xiè	_____	债券	zhài quàn	_____
煽动	shān dòng	_____	削弱	xuē ruò	_____
滋长	zī zhǎng	_____	杜绝	dù jǘe	_____
裁减	caí jiǎn	_____	捕捞	bǔ lāo	_____
归咎	guī jiù	_____	淘汰	táo tài	_____
一蹴而就	yí cù ér jiù	_____	大肆	dà sì	_____

臭名昭著 chòu míng zhāo zhù　　_____

应运而生 yīng yùn ér shēng　　_____

二、阅读理解 Reading Comprehension

1. Which year did the Chinese Exclusion Act come into force?

        A. 1855   B. 1858

        C. 1876   D. 1882

2. How many years was the Chinese Exclusion Act in existence?

        A. 50   B. 61

        C. 90   D. 100

3. Who was a labor leader of the Workingmen's Party of California?

        A. Denis Kearney   B. Benjamin Butler

C. Carl Browne   D. James Bryce

4．What were the things that the Chinese Exclusion Act prevented Chinese people from doing?

A．They were not allowed to get married.

B．They were not allowed to keep the queue.

C．They were not allowed to use shoulder poles.

D．Both B and C.

5．What effect did the Chinese Exclusion Act o to the Chinese at that time?

A．They felt protected   B．They were insulted

C．They were interested   D．They felt respected

三、电子邮件 E-mail Response

Read this e-mail from a friend and then type a response.

Simplified Character Version	Traditional Character Version
发件人：珊珊 邮件主题：是否继续做助教？	寄件者：珊珊 郵件主題：是否繼續做助教？
我从九年级开始周末一直在中文学校双语班做助教，与老师和小同学们建立了良好的关系。但是妈妈告诉我，上 11 年级后就不要去	我從九年級開始週末一直在中文學校雙語班做助教，與老師和小同學們建立了良好的關係。但是媽媽告訴我，上 11 年級後就

70

做助教了，因为学习任务很紧张，必须为报考一所好大学做准备。但是我觉得做助教是非常开心的事情，不知道怎样选择才好？	不要去做助教了，因為學習任務很緊張，必須為報考一所好大學做準備。但是我覺得做助教是非常開心的事情，不知道怎樣選擇才好？

四、写作训练 Writing Practice

尽量应用以下的成语，从时间、地点、人物事件和影响等方面复述旧金山暴动。

脱颖而出 to stand out　　　不计其数 countless

兴高采烈 in high spirits; excited

无地自容 to feel extremely ashamed

无所作为 not to be able to accomplish something

_____

_____

_____

_____

_____

_____

Reference：
美华史记 | 加州工人党和 "排华法案"
https://mp.weixin.qq.com/s/PGBC90ez-aJBq5KSkFofCQ

The Workingmen's Party of California and the Chinese Exclusion Act

Translated by Rebecca Kuang

During the late Qing dynasty, China's national power was collapsing, and its people were struggling to make a living. The Western great powers coined the term "Yellow Peril" to incite fear and hatred against the Chinese among their citizens.

In American history, the years between 1873 to 1878 was a time of severe economic depression. In 1877, a period of vast unemployment, the Workingmen's Party of California seized their opportunity to rise. That year, they took control of the California state legislature, gaining the power to amend the state constitution. Denis Kearney, a labor leader of the Workingmen's Party, believed that the Chinese were "slaves of cheap labor." He believed that their labor had eroded the living standards of Americans, and that they ought to be deported from the United States. He wantonly exploited racist ideas to push out and marginalize Chinese immigrants.

Indeed, during the economic recession, employers were more willing to retain the cheaper Chinese workers while laying off white workers in order to reduce costs. As a result, whites blamed the Chinese for their unemployment.

Unable to vent their frustrations, the public was quickly stirred up by Kearney's racist ideas. For no reason at all, they began to support all kinds of anti-Chinese actions. On 23 July 1877, shocking riots broke out in San

Francisco. Over two days, white people led large-scale mass riots targeted against the Chinese.

On this day, the Workingmen's Party of the United States convened a special meeting. About 8,000 people from all over the United States poured into the San Francisco City Hall. The Workingmen's Party leaders pinned the problem of unemployment on Chinese immigrants, thus triggering the fuse that set off the volcano of resentment that had been bubbling over this wave of unemployment. Large masses of people rushed into Chinatown like a river that had burst its banks and madly carried out a two-day rampage of vandalism and looting. This led to the deaths of four Chinese people. Twenty Chinese-owned laundromats were destroyed. The losses from damage exceeded $100,000.

On the night of July 24, the racially-charged violence was finally curbed thanks to the effort of the police, state militia, and a thousand members of the citizens' vigilance committee. Kearney, in a surprising turn of events, rose to prominence due to his efforts to quell the disturbance. From this moment, he began to promote the anti-Chinese movement in America and helped to facilitate the infamous Chinese Exclusion Act (An Act to Execute Certain Treaty Stipulations Relating to the Chinese) that Congress passed on 6 May 1882.

After the Chinese Exclusion Act was passed, the Chinese were knocked to the lowest rungs of society. There began a large number of violent attacks against the Chinese in the United States, particularly in the northwest. However, the Chinese Exclusion Act was not created overnight. More than thirty years before the law was passed, there were already a number of unreasonable laws and provisions targeting the Chinese.

For example, in 1850, California levied a tax against foreign mining. "Foreign" principally meant Chinese miners and mining sites. In 1852 Commutation Tax required shipmasters to prepare a list of foreign passengers and ship owners to post a $500 bond for each, which could be commuted by paying a tax of $5 to $50 per passenger. The law was an attempt to dissuade Chinese immigration. During the California Gold Rush, 20,026 Chinese workers came to the United States to serve as cheap labor in the arduous gold mining industry. However, the tax on foreign mining rose from $3 to $4, and many mining sites prohibited Chinese miners. In 1854, the California Supreme Court ruled that the Chinese were not permitted to testify against white citizens. In 1855, California passed a bill to "discourage the immigration to this state of persons who cannot become citizens thereof." In some Californian counties, a "naturalization tax" of $25 was levied on every person who was not eligible to become a citizen (which meant, of course, the Chinese). In addition, transporting Chinese immigrants required a "capitation tax" of $50 per immigrant.

In 1858, California passed an act legally prohibiting Chinese and "Mongolian" immigration. In 1860, the San Francisco city hospital stopped accepting Chinese patients. Public schools in northern California refused to admit Chinese students. In 1866, this law was revised to allow Chinese students to attend school with white students if the white parents did not object. In 1862, the thirty-seventh United States Congress passed the "Anti-Coolie" Act, which prohibited American ships from engaging in the coolie trade. In 1870, San Francisco's municipal engineering projects were prohibited from hiring Chinese workers. The city also banned the use of carrying poles for peddling vegetables. Immigration officials were allowed to determine at will whether or not female Chinese immigrants were prostitutes and to request that Chinese men demonstrate proof of good character before entering the country. That year, eight years after the "Anti-Coolie" Act was implemented, Africans were allowed to become American citizens through naturalization. However, the law continued to exclude Asians, particularly the Chinese, from citizenship. Dozens of states passed foreign land laws prohibiting non-citizens from buying real estate property. Chinese immigrants could not vote or sit on a jury they couldn't own land, and they couldn't establish permanent residences or businesses. In 1873, San Francisco implemented a quarterly tax of $15 for every laundromat that delivered clothes by pole and $2 for every laundromat that delivered clothes by car. That year, San Francisco also restricted the use of firecrackers and ceremonial gongs at Chinese festivals. In 1875, San Francisco passed an anti-queue law, and anyone who did not cut their queues was arrested and sent to prison. San Francisco also required that every residential room have at least 500 cubic feet of open space in order to prevent poor Chinese residents from cramming into small apartments. In 1875, California passed a regulation on the size of shrimp nets to cut down on the number of Chinese fishers.

Legislation passed in 1876 gave the federal government absolute authority over immigration legislation. In 1879, the California state constitution prohibited companies and municipal projects from hiring Chinese people. The Chinese were restricted to specific areas outside the city borders. In 1880, San Francisco passed an anti-ironing ordinance to prohibit laundromats from operating at night. California also passed the Fishing Act in 1880, which prohibited Chinese people from engaging in any fishing activity. The Burlingame Treaty of 1868 was amended in the Angell Treaty, thus restricting immigration of Chinese laborers to the United

States. In 1882, San Francisco passed the New Laundry Licensing Act, requiring all Chinese-owned laundromats to obtain a permit. The California state legislature declared a legal holiday to allow the public to attend anti-Chinese demonstrations. That same year, the Chinese Exclusion Act was officially passed and made law.

During this decade, the Chinese were actually doing the work that white workers refused to, such as panning gravel, plowing land, opening laundromats and restaurants, working as domestic helpers, etc. However, the moment white Americans began losing their jobs, they believed that the Chinese had stolen the job opportunities they hadn't even wanted. They saw themselves as a "superior" race and felt ashamed to even work side-by-side with the Chinese. During this period, the momentum of white Americans' frenzied drive for revenge grew, and race riots and clashes were frequent. In 1871, violence broke out in Los Angeles, and between 17 and 20 Chinese were lynched in one night. After the Chinese Exclusion Act had been in effect for 20 years, the United States Congress added legal provisions to more directly restrict the naturalization of Chinese immigrants.

Over the next long sixty-one years, Chinese Americans lived under the shadow of an unfair, undemocratic law. The Chinese Exclusion Act was not repealed until 1943 and not completely abolished until 1965.

地狱谷惨案

改编：潘秋辰
原创：苏欣、黄倩

一百三十多年前，广东一带家境贫寒的华人，历尽艰辛，远渡重洋，前往美国挣钱养家。他们来到美国时，身无分文，唯一拥有的便是吃苦耐劳的天性和卖苦力的身板。

当时他们大多受雇于早期到达美国，稍微有了一些根基的华人开办的公司。他们一心想挣够了钱就回到故乡过安稳的生活，然而，他们没想到，许多人却死在了异国他乡，这其中就有三十四名普通华工死于地狱谷屠杀。

爱达荷州(Idaho)与俄勒冈州(Oregon)的分界线上有一条河叫蛇河(Snake River)，河流流经一个山谷叫地狱谷(Hells Canyon)。1887 年，是《关于执行有关华人条约诸规定的法律》 (即"排华法案")正式生效的第五年。这一年春天，积雪消融后，人们在路易斯顿(Lewiston)南的蛇河上发现了一具尸体，很快，人们在河下游，相继发现了第二具、第三具尸体。接下来的几天里，死亡谷又现出四具尸体，前后总共发现 34 名华人遇害。

《路易斯顿快报》很快报道了这件事。两周后，当地检察官文森特(J.K. Vincent)和一个中国商人前往现场查看，有的尸体显然遭受过残酷的折磨，胸部中枪，臂膀被肢解，头与身体几乎分离等惨状令人惊异。

蛇河是爱达荷州与俄勒冈州的天然分界线，河流经过的这个山谷叫地狱谷。The Snake River is the natural dividing line between Idaho and Oregon. The valley that the river passes through is called the Hells Canyon. TopoView of Hells Canyon, United States. Courtesy of the U.S. Geological Survey.

华人死亡的消息很快就传播开来，人们对这个结果似乎早有预期。刚开始华工在这里备受欢迎，因为修筑太平洋铁路进展缓慢，所以铁路公司才雇佣了大批华工。吃苦耐劳的华工将铁路修完后，用所得的血汗钱开餐馆，经营洗衣店，生意逐渐红火起来。

华人在劳力市场的竞争力大大打击了白人劳工赖以生存的环境，白人开始采用各种手段夺取好的金矿地盘，并驱赶华人。华人在白人遗弃的金矿淘金，或者到最凶险的地区开辟出新矿区，一些华工冒着生命危险到地狱谷去淘金，白人非常仇恨华人这种生存能力，以至于这种仇恨给华工带来了灾难。

检察官文森特出具了一份现场调查报告，并交给了中国使馆。华人开办的三邑(Sam Yup)公司拿出 1000 美元悬赏凶手，还雇佣了调查员李来(音译，

Lee Loi)参与调查。驻美公使张荫桓1888年给美国政府前后写了近24封抗议暴行，要求查处凶手的信函，至今尚保存完好。

但是当时警方并不认为杀害了华人是什么大不了的事情，而且当地人都知道这场针对华人的杀戮是公开的，凶手就是 32 岁的埃文斯(Bruce Evans)、21 岁的坎菲尔德(J. Titus Canfield)、20 岁的拉鲁(Omar LaRue)、37 岁的休斯(Carl Hughes)、38 岁的梅纳德(Hiram Maynard)、15 岁的麦克米兰(Robert McMillan)、18 岁的沃恩(Frank Vaughan)等当地白人。

凶手麦克米兰的父亲在 1891 年临终前忏悔时说出，这伙人第一天先开枪杀死了 12 个人，第二天，他们在一艘船上杀死8名华工，随后乘船前往 4 英里外杀死了另外13名华人。最后一名华工跳上船想逃跑，也被他们用石头砸死。他们抛尸入河，抢走华工们淘来的金子。这与社会历史学家芬德利(Ross Findley)描述的情景一致：农场主克雷格(George S. Craig)提供了木屋供凶手隐藏作案。凶手们互相配合，备马、放哨、射杀，用来福枪连续杀死了 34 名华人，一个接一个像杀狗一样。

假如被杀的 34 人是白人，法律一定会惩治凶手。可惜死者都是中国人，没人认识他们，也没人在乎他们，所以后来这些凶手都被法庭释放了。

2017 年 3 月，美国华工历史学家何翠媚女士通过在旧金山总部的三邑公司，查阅了当年信件，找到公司下属十名遇害华工的中文名字，他们是来自一个村子的谢姓宗亲，但其余24 名遇害的华工，至今无从查询。

有着 40 年职业记者生涯的作家诺克斯(R. Gregory Nokes)曾随美国总统里根访问过中国。作为俄勒冈州土生土长的人，他甚至根本不了解这件历史上惊人的屠杀案。诺克斯用了近十年的时间去调查，并证明当地官员将记载了屠杀案的重要文件隐藏在了地下室废弃的柜子里，凶手远亲马丁(Marjorie Martin)以及霍纳(Harley Horner)和巴特利特(Grace Bartlett)共同完成这一时期的县志时，根本没有提及这件屠杀案。1888 年 8 月 31 日的凶犯庭审记录，竟然是一张空白纸。

马丁是"秘密守护者"之一，凶手的远亲。瓦洛瓦(Wallowa)县的资深职员承认他们隐瞒了大屠杀和审判的记录。Marjorie Martin was one of the secret keepers, the murderer's distant relatives. The Long-time Wallowa County clerk acknowledged hiding records of the massacre and trial. Photo courtesy of R. Gregory Nokes.

1983 年斯特拉顿(David H. Stratton)在其论文中写到：美国西部发生的暴力排华事件中，地狱谷蛇河屠杀案的残暴程度是无案可及的，这是美国历史上白人对华人最惨烈的一场屠杀，然而历史纪录上却不写此事，惨案地点也没有标牌。

1936 年建的荣誉墙位于瓦洛瓦县法院。荣誉墙上深深地刻着先驱功臣、杀人犯埃文斯。
View of the Wallowa County Courthouse with a memorial arch dedicated to the county's earliest settlers. The plaque with the name of E.E. Evans, the leader of a gang of horse thieves accused of murders. Photo courtesy of Gary Halvorson, Oregon State Archives.

　　诺克斯经过大量调查研究，于 2009 年出版了"偷窃黄金大屠杀：地狱峡
谷华人"这本书。 之后，诺克斯和一组志愿者组织了地狱峡谷华人纪念委员
会，让人们记住长期被隐藏的罪行。联邦政府已将该地点正式指定为华人大
屠杀湾。

为了纪念被谋杀的中国人，诺克斯和其他志愿者在位于距离爱达荷州刘易斯顿以南 65 英里的大屠杀现场安装了纪念碑。Memorial to the murdered Chinese, installed by Mr. Nokes and other volunteers at the site of the massacre, 65 miles south of Lewiston, Idaho. Photo courtesy of R. Gregory Nokes.

练 习

一、生词 New Words：请为文中下列词语标注上拼音。

家境贫寒 _____   远渡重洋 _____

历尽艰辛 _____   身无分文 _____

赖以生存 _____   吃苦耐劳 _____

异国他乡 _____   积雪消融 _____

受雇 _____   安稳 _____

地狱	_____	屠杀	_____
残酷	_____	折磨	_____
肢解	_____	惨状	_____
雇佣	_____	驱赶	_____
遗弃	_____	凶险	_____
仇恨	_____	灾难	_____
抗议	_____	信函	_____
杀戮	_____	忏悔	_____
隐藏	_____	放哨	_____
惩治	_____	释放	_____
宗亲	_____	查询	_____
记载	_____	废弃	_____
暴力	_____	标牌	_____

二、**Drills and Practice**：请注意文中有以下字词的句子，并用该字词造一个句子。

（一）和

两周后，当地检察官文森特和一个中国商人前往现场查看。

_____

（二）就

华人死亡的消息很快就传播开来，人们对这个结果似乎早有预期。

（三）才

因为修筑太平洋铁路进展缓慢，所以铁路公司才雇佣了大批华工。

（四）但是

但是当时警方并不认为杀害了华人是什么大不了的事情。

（五）然而

然而历史纪录上却不写此事，惨案地点也没有标牌。

三、阅读理解 Reading Comprehension：请讨论回答以下问题。

（一）文中提到的"地狱谷惨案"发生在什么地方？

（二）"地狱谷惨案"总共死了多少人？

（三）为什么当时警察不给凶手判刑，让他坐牢？

（四）"地狱谷惨案"中遇害的人都有名字记录吗？

_____

（五）如果你生活在惨案发生的年代，你会怎么办？

_____

四、请分组表演以下情景对话

珊珊：嘉明，听我父母说，你爷爷在很早以前就到美国来了，是吗？

嘉明：是的，那是很多年前的事情了。

珊珊：你听过爷爷讲他们那个年代的故事吗？

嘉明：爷爷给我讲过他们开洗衣房的故事。

珊珊：能给我讲讲吗？

嘉明：我不一定能讲清楚，记得爷爷说他们开洗衣房很辛苦，有时候还要被欺负。

珊珊：是啊，我们在《美华史记》里了解到很多这样的故事。

嘉明：我还记得爷爷说过，在他很小的时候，有很多同村的人来美国修铁路的事。

珊珊：不如我们向老师建议，请你爷爷到班上来给我们讲讲他们当年的故事吧，你觉得怎么样？

嘉明：好啊，不过我爷爷现在快 90 岁了，他讲话大家能听明白吗？

珊珊：没关系，只要他老人家身体允许，可以慢慢讲，我的中文水平比较好，可以帮忙解释或翻译。

嘉明：这太好啦，我们赶紧向老师申请吧。

珊珊：好的。

五、写作训练 Writing Practice

您有机会为中国学生计划蛇河和地狱谷之旅。在演示文稿中，描述一下场景，还要解释要看什么，为什么要去那里。You have an opportunity to plan a tour of the Snake River and Hells Canyon for Chinese students. In your presentation, describe the site and explain what you would do and why.

_____

_____

_____

_____

_____

_____

_____

_____

_____

References:
1. Massacred For Gold, The Chinese In The Hells Canyon by R. Gregory Nokes. Oregon State University Press.
2. 美华史记 | 地狱谷的百年悲鸣
http://mp.weixin.qq.com/s/e7DO8YtRUoqbC5tEci8SDQ

The Hells Canyon Massacre

Translated by Rebecca Kuang

More than a hundred-thirty years ago, a group of poverty-stricken Chinese immigrants from Guangdong made the long and arduous journey across the ocean to the United States in order to make money to support their families. When they arrived on America's shores, they were penniless. The only assets they had were their willingness to work diligently and endure hardship and their physical capability for hard labor.

At the time, most of them were employed by a few companies opened by Chinese people who had earlier arrived in the United States and had established some footing. They wanted to earn just enough money to return to their hometowns to live the rest of their lives in peace. However, none of them knew that many of their number would perish overseas. Among these were the thirty-four Chinese laborers who died in the Hells Canyon Massacre.

On the border between Idaho and Oregon is a river called Snake River which flows through a canyon named Hells Canyon. In 1887, the Chinese Exclusion Act (An Act to Execute Certain Treaty Stipulations Relating to the Chinese) had just been in effect for five years. In the spring of that year, after the snow had melted, a corpse was found on the Snake River bank south of Lewiston. Very soon, a second, and then a third corpse was discovered further downstream. Over the next few days, four more corpses were found in the canyon. In the end, thirty-four Chinese victims were discovered to have been murdered.

The Lewiston Teller quickly reported this incident. Two weeks later, the local prosecutor J.K. Vincent and a Chinese merchant began to investigate the crime scene. Several corpses displayed signs of cruel torture. The bodies were in a shocking state–the victims had been shot in the chest, their arms had been dismembered, and their heads separated from their bodies.

The news of the deaths quickly spread. People seemed to have expected this outcome. In the beginning, Chinese laborers had been welcomed in the United States. Because the little progress was made on building the Pacific Railroad, the railroad company started hiring large numbers of Chinese laborers. After the hardworking Chinese laborers had finished their work on the railroad, they used their hard-earned money to open restaurants and laundromats. Slowly, their lives became prosperous.

However, the labor market competitiveness of the Chinese began to greatly affect the living environment of white Americans. White Americans began using all sorts of different tactics to seize good gold mining territory and drive away the Chinese miners. The Chinese mined either in the areas that the white miners had already abandoned or in new but treacherous and dangerous mining sites. Some Chinese miners risked their lives to go to Hells Canyon to pan for gold. White miners hated these Chinese miners' will to survive. This hatred would bring disaster to the Chinese miners.

Prosecutor J.K. Vincent issued a report of the crime scene investigation to the Chinese consulate. The Chinese-owned business Sam Yup Company offered 1,000 dollars as a bounty for the murderers and hired investigator Lee Loi to make further inquiries. In 1888, Chinese ambassador Yinhuan Zhang wrote close to 24 letters protesting this atrocity and requesting criminal investigation of the murderers. These letters have been preserved to this day and are in good condition.

However, the police at the time did not view the murder of Chinese victims as anything terrible. The locals knew that this atrocity was an open act targeting the Chinese. The murderers were 32-year-old Bruce Evans, 21-year-old J. Titus Canfield, 20-year-old Omar LaRue, 37-year-old Carl Hughes, 38-year-old Hiram Maynard, 15-year-old Robert McMillan, and 18-year-old Frank Vaughan. All of them were white men from the local area.

In 1981, the father of Robert McMillan, one of the murderers, confessed on his deathbed that the gang had shot and killed twelve people on the first day of the massacre. On the second day, they killed eight Chinese laborers on a boat, traveled by ship for over four miles, and then killed another thirteen Chinese victims. At the end, one Chinese laborer jumped on the boat to flee, but the murderers stoned him to death. They robbed their Chinese victims of their gold and threw their corpses into the river. This is consistent with the account of social historian Ross Findley: rancher George S. Craig's cabin had been used by the gang to hide their criminal activities. Together, the murderers had coordinated to prepare their horses and set sentries. They had shot thirty-four Chinese victims in succession, one after the other as if they were killing dogs.

If the thirty-four victims had been white, the law certainly would have punished the murderers. But the victims were all Chinese. No one knew them, and no one cared about them. In the end, all of the murderers were set free by the court.

In March of 2017, Professor Chuimei Ho, who was researching the history of Chinese laborers, consulted records at the Sam Yup Company's headquarters in San Francisco. She found the names of ten victims in a letter from that year. They were members of the Xie clan and had come from the same village. However, the identities of the remaining twenty-four Chinese victims are unknown to this day.

R. Gregory Nokes, an author who had worked as a journalist for forty years, had once accompanied President Reagan on a visit to China. Although he had grown up in Oregon, he had never learned of this shocking massacre. Nokes, who spent close to ten years conducting research, discovered that records of the crime were hidden in an unused safe. When Marjorie Martin (a distant relative of one of the murderers), Harley Horner, and Grace Bartlett wrote a local history of that period, they made no mention of the massacre. The record for the murder court hearings on 31 August 1888 was nothing more than blank paper.

In 1983, Professor David H. Stratton wrote in an essay that the brutality of the Snake River atrocity was probably unmatched, whether by whites or Indians, in all the anti-Chinese violence of the American West. This was one of the most inhumane massacres by white Americans against the Chinese in American history. But this incident was not written into the records of history, and nor did the site of the massacre bear any mark testifying to what had happened.

After conducting a great deal of research, Mr. Nokes published the book *Massacred for Gold: The Chinese in Hells Canyon* in 2009. Afterwards, Mr. Nokes and a group of volunteers organized a Hells Canyon Chinese memorial committee, which installed a monument at the site of the massacre 65 miles from Lewiston, Idaho. This monument would let people remember this crime that had been hidden for so long.

拒戴"狗牌"：十一万人的抗争

改编：潘秋辰

原创：苏 欣

1892 年 5 月 5 日，在《关于执行有关华人条约诸规定的法律》(即"排华法案")实施十年之后，美国国会通过了《吉尔里法案》(The Geary Act)。

该法案更进一步要求每个华人居民都要随身携带证件，证件上必须有对五官、发际、下巴、头部等有严格要求的照片，以及姓名、年龄、住址、职业等个人私密信息，注册时还需要两位白人证人。如发现未携带证件者，将会被逮捕并被强迫劳动，并在一年后驱逐出境。同时，华人不具有在法庭上作证的资格，不具有保释权利。

顿时，这项法案被华人称为"狗牌法"，大家觉得所谓的身份卡是一种人格的侮辱。清政府的特派公使和全权大使崔国因在法案签署当日就曾向詹姆斯·吉莱斯皮·布莱恩(James Gillespie Blaine)国务卿提出了抗议。清朝驻旧金山副领事欧阳庆呈请清政府予以干预。

1892 年 9 月 19 日中华总会馆①号召全美 11 万华人移民每人捐款一美

元作为聘请律师的费用，与政府对簿公堂。一时间，全国各地唐人街的墙

壁和窗户上贴满了宣传此事的红色传单。

在旧金山西部以外的新英格兰、纽约，及南方地区也加入了抵抗运动。

纽约的华人平等权利联盟(Chinese Equal Rights League)招募到 150 名会说

英语的华裔商人和专业人士提出共同诉求，这一行动还得到了美国东岸不少

白人的支持，在 9 月 22 日两百名华裔商人和劳工的抗议集会中，竟然有一

千多名美国公民也加入了支持行列。伊利诺伊州共和党众议员罗伯特·西特

(Robert Hitt)谴责该法案让人类退回到了奴隶制时代。

另外，中华总会馆对一些为政府登记提供翻译服务的华商予以严厉警告

及惩处。有一些餐馆或肉店老板去注册登记了，中华总会馆就以他们违背了

卫生条令给予惩罚。中华总会馆和太平洋航运公司还商定，每个乘船华人只

有带上坚持拒绝登记身份卡的通知，才可以登船。

加利福尼亚麻纺厂威胁要开除不办卡的华人雇员，中华总会馆随即组织

华人罢工，挫败了美国税务局企图进行秘密登记的阴谋。白人报纸在报道中

挑唆说华人奴性不改，甘愿做中华总会馆的奴隶。

1893 年 3 月，旧金山税务局宣告 5 月 5 日截止日前，不按时登记的华

人将一律被抓捕。但是 4 月份，市政府暂停了登记证上贴照片的要求，白人

证人也只需要一位了。尽管做出了让步，大多数华人还是拒绝登记。

截止日期只剩下几天时，中华总会馆仍然不放心，再次提出公告，号召华人坚持抗争，禁止华人服从规定去登记"狗牌"。局势变得异常紧张起来，华人生命受到了排华势力的严重威胁。

中华总会馆。苏欣拍摄。Chinese Consolidated Benevolent Association. Photo by Xin Su.

5月5日星期五下午登记停止。税务局宣告华人登记人数：旧金山2000人(总人数28,000人)，圣地亚哥15人，洛杉矶103人(总人数5000人)，芝加哥945人(总人数2500)，以及萨克拉门托有少数人。由于有组织、有纪律，美国华人集体抵制歧视性法律的努力取得了巨大成功。全国只有3,169人注册了，而且去注册的华人包括一些妇女是为了给自己和子女提供所谓的合法保护，迫不得已而为之。

后来，僵持中的清政府为了两国之间的贸易放弃了对旅美侨胞的保护，

美国政府又延长了半年登记期限。1894 年 4 月 3 日是合法移民身份登记的

最后日子，数千人等候着中华总会馆的指示，是继续抵抗？还是前去登记？

最后失去清政府靠山的中华总会馆无奈贴出通告，劝告所有劳工遵守《吉尔

里法案》。

自 1896 年至 1905 年旅居美国的 11 万华人中，9571 人因非法居留而被

捕，4000 人被遣返。

华人渴望融入美国社会，主张与所有其他族裔享有"共同人性"，拥有

共同的平等地位。在当年疯狂排华的恶劣政治环境下，11 万华人提出了一个

平等的模式：华人与白人在社区里共存的愿景。

黄金德是一位在美国出生的华裔。1895 年去中国探望父母之后被拒绝再次回美。他将官司
打到美国最高法院，最终争取到华人的美国出生公民权。United States v. Wong Kim Ark, 169
U.S. 649 (1898) is a United States Supreme Court case that established an important precedent
in its interpretation of the Citizenship Clause of the Fourteenth Amendment to the Constitution.
Courtesy of the National Archives, Pacific Region, San Bruno, California. Ⓔ

一、注解 Notes

① 中华总会馆(Chinese Consolidated Benevolent Association)其旧金山分会的前身，也称六大公司或六大会馆。由宁阳总会馆、合和总会馆、冈州总会馆、阳和总会馆、三邑总会馆、人和总会馆组成。后来肇庆总会馆加入，增为七大会馆。

二、生词 New Words：请为文中下列词语标注上拼音。

招募 to recruit _____   惩处 punishment _____

谴责 to condemn _____   挫败 to defeat _____

严厉 strict _____   僵持 standoff _____

迫不得已 have to _____

挑唆 instigation, provocation _____

对簿公堂　to go to court _____

驱逐 the expulsion of _____
(Driven Out，Jean Pfaelzer 所著的一本书)

三、Drills and Practice：请注意文中有以下字词的句子，并用该字词造一个句子。

(一) 如……将……

如发现未携带证件者，将会被逮捕并被强迫劳动。

_____

(二) 只有......而且......

全国只有 3,169 人注册了，而且去注册的华人包括一些妇女为了给自己和子女提供所谓的合法保护，迫不得以而为之。

(三) 只有......才......

每个乘船华人只有带上坚持拒绝登记身份卡的通知，才可以登船。

(四) 尽管......还是......

尽管做出了让步，大多数华人还是拒绝登记。

(五) 是......还是......

数千人等候着中华总会馆的指示，是继续抵抗？还是前去登记？

四、阅读理解 Reading Comprehension

1. How many years after the implementation of the Chinese Exclusion Act was the Geary Act introduced?

      A. 40   B. 30

      C. 20   D. 10

2. Why were Chinese people not willing to wear identity cards?

A. Because it was too much trouble.

B. Because it was not pretty.

C. Because it was too loud.

D. Because they were insulted.

3. Why did the Qing government not support the American emigrants to resist the Geary Act?

A. Because the U.S. government apologized.

B. Because the Chinese nationals all returned home.

C. Because the Geary Act was repealed.

D. Because of the economic and trade benefits.

4. What kind of organization is the Chinese Consolidated Benevolent Association?

A. It is an overseas department of the Qing government.

B. It is a non-governmental organization for Chinese Americans.

C. It's an army.

D. It is a rich man.

5. Which of the following is true?

A. The collective resistance of 110,000 Chinese Americans to the defeat of the Geary Act was because some women had conceded to the government.

B. The Qing government abandoned the American emigrants because they had all become naturalized.

C. Chinese Americans wanted to fight the Geary Act, but not by legal means.

D. The collective resistance of 110,000 Chinese against the Geary Act failed, but it was a successful step towards the repeal of the Chinese Exclusion Act.

五、写作训练 Writing Practice

请观察以下图片，了解华人身份卡那段历史，写写你心里想说的话。

图片一、Certificate of residence for Wong Kin Hay [?]/Certificates of residence for Chinese laborers, MS 3642. Courtesy of the California Historical Society. Ⓒ

*****

References：

1. 美华史记｜排华法案的第二个十年
http://mp.weixin.qq.com/s/GA-EKEe8l4HCgf7DabhMew
2. Driven Out: The Forgotten War against Chinese Americans by Jean Pfaelzer. University of California Press.

图片二、Certificate of residence for Ju Sing/Certificates of residence for Chinese laborers, MS 3642. Courtesy of the California Historical Society. Ⓔ

图片三、Certificate of residence for Lung Tang/Certificates of residence for Chinese laborers, MS 3642. Courtesy of the California Historical Society. Ⓔ

图片四、Geary Exclusion Act by George Yost Coffin (1850-1896). Courtesy of the Library of Congress. ⊘

The 110,000 Who Defied the "Dog Tag Law"

Translated by Rebecca Kuang

On 5 May 1892, ten years after the Chinese Exclusion Act (An Act to Execute Certain Treaty Stipulations Relating to the Chinese) became law, the United States Congress passed the Geary Act.

This act required every Chinese resident in the United States to carry identification cards on their persons at all times. The identification cards had to include a photo with strict requirements for display of facial features including the hairline, chin, and crown. They also had to include private information such as last name, age, address, and occupation. When registering, Chinese residents also needed two white people to be present as witnesses. If anyone was found without identification, they would be arrested, sentenced to forced labor, and deported a year later. At the same time, the Chinese were not permitted to testify in court and did not have the right to be released on bail.

The Chinese immediately began referring to this act as the "Dog Tag Law." They believed that being forced to carry identification at all times was an insult to their personal dignity. Cui Guoyin, the Qing government's foreign minister and plenipotentiary ambassador, expressed his dissatisfaction to Secretary of State James Gillespie Blaine on the day the bill was signed. Ouyang Qing, the vice consul at the Chinese consulate in San Francisco, submitted a request to the Qing government to intervene.

On 19 September 1892, the Chinese Consolidated Benevolent Association (the Chinese Six Companies) called for all 110,000 Chinese immigrants in the United States to contribute one dollar in order to raise funds to hire a lawyer to sue the federal government. For a brief moment, every wall and window on the streets of Chinatowns all over the country were covered with red propaganda pamphlets publicizing this matter.

Areas outside San Francisco including New England, New York, and the South joined in the resistance movement. The Chinese Equal Rights League of New York recruited 150 English-speaking Chinese businessmen and professionals to join its cause. This movement won the support of many white people on the east coast. On September 22, more than one thousand American citizens joined a protest rally organized by two hundred Chinese businessmen and laborers. Robert Hitt, a Republican Congressional representative from Illinois, denounced the Geary Act for dragging respect for human rights back to the era of slavery.

The Chinese Consolidated Benevolent also issued stern warnings and punishments to any Chinese businesses that offered translation services for government registration efforts. Whenever a restaurant owner or butcher went to register, the Chinese Consolidated Benevolent Association penalized their businesses for violating hygiene standards. The Chinese Consolidated Benevolent Association formed an agreement with the Pacific Mail Steamship company: any Chinese person who wanted to board a boat had to carry a paper stating that they insisted on refusing to register their identity.

When California Jute Mill threatened to expel Chinese employees who did not carry identification cards, the Chinese Consolidated Benevolent Association immediately organized a labor strike, thus thwarting the Bureau of Internal Revenue's plans to carry out secret registrations. White newspapers provocatively described the Chinese as slaves who bent to do the will of the Chinese Consolidated Benevolent Association.

In March 1893, the Collector of Internal Revenue in San Francisco announced that any Chinese people who had not registered by the May 5 would be arrested. But by April, the city suspended the photo requirements for identification cards. They also changed the testifying requirement to just one white witness. Despite the city's concessions, many Chinese people still refused to register.

A few days before the May 5 deadline, the Chinese Consolidated Benevolent Association was still worried, and again posted announcements calling for Chinese people to persevere in their resistance. They forbade Chinese people to obey the Geary Act and register for "dog tags". The situation turned extremely intense, and anti-Chinese forces seriously threatened Chinese lives.

Registration closed on May 5. The Bureau of Internal Revenue released the following numbers of Chinese registration: 2000 people registered in San Francisco (out of a total of 28,000 people), 15 people registered in San Diego, 103 people registered in Los Angeles (out of a total of 5,000 people), 945 people registered in Chicago (out of a total of

2,500 people), and a few registered in Sacramento. Because of their organization and discipline, the Chinese across America had succeeded in banding together and boycotting the racist law. Only 3,169 Chinese people registered across the entire country. The Chinese who did go register included women who were forced to do so in order to ensure legal protections for their children.

In the end, the deadlocked Qing government gave up protections for overseas Chinese to mantain its trade relations with the United States. The US government extended the registration deadline by six months. April 3, 1894 was the final day of legal immigrant registration. Over a thousand people waited for directions from the Chinese Consolidated Benevolent Association. Were they going to continue their protest? Or should they follow the law and register? At last, the Chinese Consolidated Benevolent Association, which had lost the support of the Qing government, had no choice but to post a notice announcing that laborers were advised to go ahead and obey the Geary Act.

Between 1896 and 1906, of the 110,000 Chinese people in the United States, 9,571 were arrested for illegal residence, and 4,000 were deported back to China.

Chinese people longed to assimilate into American society. They claimed a common manhood and advocated for equal status with all other nationalities. Under the harsh political environment formed by the madness of the anti-Chinese movement, 110,000 Chinese people proposed a model of equality: a vision of coexistence between white and Chinese people in the same community.

王清福：美国华人第一人

骆 西

"当你不投票或者不愿意去投票时，政治人物就会拿你当条爬虫；一旦你来到投票箱前，他们就会拿你当人看，拿你当兄弟，并用雪茄、威士忌和啤酒来将你款待。"——王清福

王清福。Wong Chin Foo, a notable Chinese lecturer. Photo by Rookwood. Harper's Weekly (May 26, 1877).

同学们，读了上面这段话你有什么感想呢？这句话正是出自本篇故事的主角王清福。他当之无愧可以称得上"美国华人第一人"①。因为 Chinese American，美国华人或华裔美国人②，这个词正是他首创的。在没有这个称呼之前，华人在美国即使获得了美国国籍，依然被叫做华人(Chinese)。王清福是在美国最早被大众(public)认识的华人。他创办报纸、组织社团、用英语写作、演讲(speech)，为华人争取权利(rights)。他的一生很好地履行了作为美国华人(Chinese American)的双重使命(dual duties)——为了华人的权利和实现一个真正自由平等的美国(free and equal)而战。

王清福 1847 年出生在山东一个富裕的家庭。可是父亲不善管理财产，父子俩最后竟成了乞丐(beggar)。1861 年，王清福 14 岁那年遇见在山东传教的赫尔姆斯(Landrum and Sallie Holmes)夫妇。这对美国夫妇不光收留了王清福，还在 1867 年带他来到美国，希望他日后成为传教士。在美国，王清福先后在华盛顿特区的哥伦比亚学院(今乔治华盛顿大学)和宾夕法尼亚州的路易斯伯格学院(Lewisburg,今巴克奈尔大学)学习。在读书期间，王清福去了很多城市演讲。他地道的(genuine)英语，幽默的(humorous)演讲风格，让观众心甘情愿地掏钱听他讲中国文化和各种趣闻。毕业后，王清福在美国各地游历(travel)。

1871 年，他回到中国结婚生子。虽然他最终没有做传教士(missionary)，可是工作之余，他仍然四处演讲。1873 年，王清福因为反清③，被清政府通

^{jī}缉(list as wanted)，不得不告别妻儿，再次来到美国。他所处的年代，正好是

美国的财富迅速^{jī lěi}积累的年代——数百万^{yí mín}移民(immigrant)来到美国，大量的^{zhòng}重

^{gōng yè}工业(large-scale industry)，包括铁路、工厂、^{cǎi kuàng}采矿(mining)都飞速发展。可是，

在经济发展的同时，美国社会也存在很多黑暗面，包括政府^{fǔ bài}腐败(corruption)、

^{pín fù xuán shū}贫富悬殊、^{zhǒng zú qí shì}种族歧视等问题。1869 年美国第一条横贯东西的铁路完工之后，

大批华人失业。华工要求的工资很低。因为担心^{jiù yè jìng zhēng}就业竞争，华工被诬陷为造^{wū xiàn}

成白人工人失业的^{zuì kuí huò shǒu}罪魁祸首。在这样的历史^{bèi jǐng}背景下，王清福来到美国后成了

^{zhí yè yǎn shuō jiā}职业演说家(professional lecturer)。他在美国各地演讲，向对华人有^{piān jiàn}偏见的美

国人介绍中国文化；对恶意^{è yì zhòng shāng}中伤华人的行为给予反击。仅在 1876 年一年中，

王清福就做了 80 多场演讲。

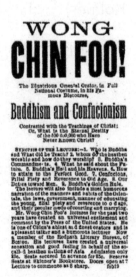

王清福的演讲广告。This advertisement for a lecture appeared in the Quincy, Illinois Daily Herald on February 19, 1878.

1882 年，在 种 族 主 义(racism)的推波助澜下，美国国会通过了《关于执行有关华人条约诸规定的法律》(即"排华法案")，停止大部分华人移民美国，让已经在美国的华人也无法取得美国国籍。1883 年夏天，当爱尔兰(Irish)政客丹尼斯·科尼(Denis Kearney)不断在演讲中说"无论如何，华人必须离开"时，王清福不光跟他在报纸上辩论，更要求与他决斗(duel)。王清福说，决斗的武器可以从"筷子、爱尔兰土豆或者阿姆斯特朗大砲(krupp guns)④"中选。

有言论(opinion)说"中国人没有宗教信仰(religious faith)，死后只能下地狱(go to hell)"。为此，1887 年王清福发表了一篇轰动美国的文章《为什么我是一个异教徒？》在文章中他说，儒教(孔子思想)⑤也是一种信仰。为什么一位善良的中国人仅仅因为没有听说过基督(Jesus)死后就要下地狱？

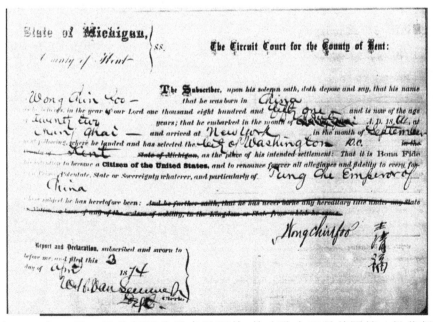

王清福于 1874 年 4 月 4 日获得了公民身份证件，他声称自己是美国第一批获得公民身份的中国人。Wong Chin Foo Naturalization Paper. Naturalization Records of the Seventeenth Circuit Court 1860-1929, Archives of Michigan.

王清福一直鼓励华人加入美国国籍、参政（cān zhèng）、投票、学英语、减掉辫子（jiǎn diào biàn zi）、穿西服，积极融入美国社会。1874 年王清福加入美国国籍，成为美国公民（měi guó gōng mín）(American citizen)。1892 年"排华法案"开始第二个十年，法案增加了更多严苛的条款（yán kē tiáo kuǎn）(stringent laws)。王清福帮助成立了"华人平等权利联盟(Chinese Equal Rights League)"，并在纽约和波士顿组织大规模抗议活动，希望推翻这一不公正的法律。

1896 年，王清福冒险回到中国与妻儿相见。在漂洋过海的旅途中，王清福筋疲力尽（jīn pí lì jìn），几个星期瘦了 20 磅。1898 年，王清福因为心力衰竭(heart failure)，在中国病逝（bìng shì）。

对于王清福丰富的人生，这篇文章只罗列（luó liè）(list)了他几个重要的经历。"人人生而平等"、"自由"与"人权"是美国建国的精神。而这些权利不应该只属于一部分人。作为"美国华人第一人"，王清福坚信（jiān xìn）这些真理（zhēn lǐ），他说："人品和才能应该是成为美国公民的条件。"为了实现这个梦，他奋斗（fèn dòu）了一生。

练 习

一、 注释 Note

① 王清福当之无愧可以称得上"美国华人第一人（dì yī rén）"。

109

第一人，既指次序上居于首位，也指才能、品德、姿容等方面最好的人。

The first person refers to the order of the first place, but also the best person in terms of talent, morality and appearance.

② 1883 年 2 月，王清福在纽约创办了"美华新报(Chinese American)"。Chinese American，美国华人或华裔美国人这个称呼由此诞生。这份报纸只维持了 7 个月。

In February 1883, Wong Chin Foo founded the *Chinese American* in New York. The title of the Chinese American was created. This newspaper lasted only for seven months.

③ 反清：anti-Manchu government. The Qing dynasty was the last imperial dynasty of China. Established in 1636, it ruled China from 1644 to 1912.

④ 克虏伯大炮(krupp guns)

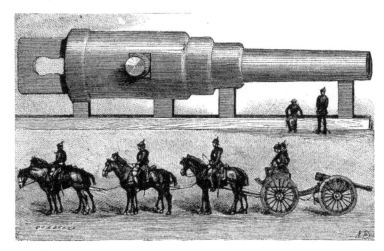

The new krupp guns (1880) in Scientific American Supplement No. 598, June 18, 1887.

⑤孔子：Confucius (551-479 BC). The philosophy of Confucius was known as Confucianism(儒教).

CONFUCIUS (c551-479 B.C.). Chinese philosopher. Gouache on paper, c1770. The Granger Collection. Encyclopedia Britannica.©

二、　　生词 New Word

投票	tóu piào	to vote
款待	kuǎn dài	to treat cordially
当之无愧	dāng zhī wú kuì	fully deserve (a title, an honor, etc.)
首创	shǒu chuàng	to initiate，首创精神 initiative
心甘情愿	xīn gān qíng yuàn	to be most willing to
趣闻	qù wén	anecdotes, interesting stories

积累	jī lěi	to accumulate 积累经验
贫富悬殊	pín fù xuán shū	polarization of the rich and the poor
就业竞争	jiù yè jìng zhēng	to compete for the post
诬陷	wū xiàn	to frame sb. up
罪魁祸首	zuì kuí huò shǒu	the chief culprit
推波助澜	tuī bō zhù lán	to help intensify the strength of billows and waves
恶意中伤	è yì zhòng shāng	to viciously slander
轰动	hōng dòng	to cause a sensation
政客	zhèng kè	politician
参政	cān zhèng	to take part in politics or the government
筋疲力尽	jīn pí lì jìn	to be completely exhausted
病逝	bìng shì	to die of an illness
真理	zhēn lǐ	truth
奋斗	fèn dòu	to strive

三、 练习与运用 Drills and practice

<u>选词填空</u>

(一) 他____报纸、____社团、用英语写作、演讲，为华人____权利。

A. 创作....组织....争取   B. 创办....组织....争取

C. 创立....经营....争夺   D. 创造....管理....争夺

112

(二) 他＿＿＿英语，＿＿＿演讲风格，让观众＿＿＿掏钱听他讲中国文化和各种趣闻。

　　A. 糟糕的....枯燥的....心甘情愿地

　　B. 地道的....枯燥的....迫不得已地

　　C. 地道的....幽默的....心甘情愿地

　　D. 地道的....幽默的....迫不得已地

请选出与文章内容一致的一项。

(三) 王清福所处的年代正好是美国的财富迅速积累的年代——数百万移民来到美国，大量的重工业，包括铁路、工厂、采矿都飞速发展。可是，在经济发展的同时，美国社会也存在很多黑暗面，包括政府腐败、贫富悬殊、种族歧视等问题。

　　A. 这个时期美国经济很差　　　B. 这个时期美国社会问题不多

　　C. 这个时期华人在美国不受歧视　　D. 这是美国工业大发展的时期

Reference：
The First Chinese American: The Remarkable Life of Wong Chin Foo by Scott D. Seligman. Hong Kong University Press.

Wong Chin Foo: The First Chinese American

Translated by Rebecca Kuang

"When you don't vote and don't wish to vote, he denounces you as a reptile; the moment you appear at the ballot box you are a man and a brother and are treated (if you consort with such people) to cigars, whiskies, and beers."——Wong Chin Foo

Dear students, what are your thoughts on the above quote? Wong Chin Foo, the main character of this story, spoke these words. He fully deserves to be called the first Chinese American because he came up with that label. Before the term existed, Chinese immigrants who had obtained American citizenship were still referred to as the Chinese. Wong Chin Foo was the first Chinese person recognized by the American public. He founded newspapers, organized societies, and used his English writings and speeches to fight for the rights of the Chinese. Throughout his life, he fulfilled the dual duties of being a good Chinese American. He fought both to protect the rights of the Chinese and to bring about a freer and equal United States.

Wong Chin Foo was born in 1847 to a wealthy family in Shandong. His father managed his wealth poorly, and the family quickly descended into poverty. In 1861, the fourteen-year-old Wong met missionaries Landrum and Sallie Holmes. The Holmeses hoped that Wong would become a missionary in the future. The Holmeses not only took Wong into their care, they brought him with them to the United States in 1867, where Wong first attended Columbian College (now named George Washington University) in Washington, D.C. and then Lewisburg College (now named Bucknell University) in Pennsylvania. While he was a student, Wong travelled to many cities to give speeches. Because of his genuine English and humorous speaking style, audiences were happy to pay to listen to him talk about Chinese culture and other topics of interest. After he graduated, Wong traveled all over the United States.

In 1871, he went back to China to marry and start a family. Although he did not become a missionary, but he spoke in many areas. By 1873 Wong was listed as wanted by the Qing government because of his anti-Qing activities. He was forced to say goodbye to his wife and child and return to the United States. This was during a time of rapid accumulation of wealth in America. Millions of immigrants came to the United States to work in large-scale industries including railroads, factories, and mining, which were all speedily taking off. However, at the same time that the economy was developing, there were also many problems in American society including corruption, wealth inequality, and racial discrimination. In 1869, after the first cross-continental railroad connecting the east and west coasts finished construction, many Chinese people lost their jobs. Chinese laborers worked for very low salaries. Because they feared job competition, white workers painted the Chinese as scapegoats for the unemployment problem. It was under these historical circumstances that Wong Chin Foo became a professional lecturer in the United States. Wong spoke all over the United States, introducing Chinese culture to Americans who held anti-Chinese prejudices and refuting the malicious slander and libel that had been launched against the Chinese. Wong gave 80 public speeches in the year 1876 alone.

In 1882, influenced by a growing racist movement, the United States Congress passed the Chinese Exclusion Act (An Act to Execute Certain Treaty Stipulations Relating to the Chinese) which halted the majority of Chinese immigration to the United States and left no way for the Chinese already living in the US to obtain American citizenship. In the summer of 1883, the Irish politician Denis Kearney was giving speech after speech declaring that, "Whatever happens, the Chinese go!" Wong not only debated with Kearney in the newspapers, he even challenged him to a duel. The weapons of choice, Wong said, "I would give him his choice of chopsticks, Irish potatoes or Krupp guns."

Some people believed that because the Chinese had no religious faith, they would go to hell after their deaths. In response, Wong published the sensational article "Why am I a Heathen?" in 1887. In the article, Wong argued that Confucianism was also a religious belief. Why would a good and honest Chinese person go to hell after death just because they hadn't heard of Jesus Christ?

Wong continued to encourage Chinese people to obtain American citizenship, participate in politics, vote, learn English, cut their queues, wear Western clothing, and actively assimilate into American society. In 1874, Wong became an American citizen. In 1892, after the Chinese Exclusion Act had been in effect for 10 years, even more stringent laws were passed on Chinese immigration. Wong helped to found the Chinese Equal Rights League, which organized mass protests in New York and Boston to overturn this unjust law.

In 1896, Wong took the risk to return home to see his wife and son. Exhausted by the overseas journey, he lost twenty pounds in several weeks. Wong passed away in China in 1898 from complications due to heart failure.

This article has covered only a few of the most important episodes of Wong's rich and fascinating life. The values of freedom, human rights, and the notion that all people are born equal form the bedrock of the American spirit. These privileges should not belong only to a fraction of the population. Wong Chin Foo, the very first Chinese American, believed firmly in this truth. As Wong once said, "Character and fitness should be the requirement of all who are desirous of becoming citizens of the American Republic." He fought his entire life to realize this dream.

******

The first page of the US Chinese Exclusion Act (An Act to execute certain treaty stipulations relating to Chinese), Enacted by the 47th United States Congress and Effective on May 6, 1882. Public law: 47-126. https://www.ourdocuments.gov/doc.php?flash=true&doc=47#

看图写作训练

根据下面这幅图回答问题：1. 这幅图里有哪些人物？2. 这些人物在干什么？3. 为什么会发生这样的事件？ 4. 通过这幅图画家想告诉我们什么？ 请同学们先查阅相关历史资料，写一篇议论文（non-fiction）。

1871年2月18日哈珀周刊上刊出纳斯特这幅插图。哥伦比亚女神呼喊着"住手，绅士们！美国意味着人人平等！" "Columbia defends disconsola[t]e John Chinaman from nativist Attacks" (February 18, 1871) by Thomas Nast. Ⓔ

_____

_____

Reference:
美华史记 | 漫画之父与华人 1：路见不平拔笔相助
http://mp.weixin.qq.com/s/cq6zW6pUDxLH5OmxmBMDBA

背景知识: 泰坦尼克号是一艘英国邮轮(yóulún), 也是当时世界上最大, 号称"永不沉没"的梦幻之船。1912 年 4 月 10 日泰坦尼克号从英国南安普敦(Southampton)出发, 4 月 14 日在到纽约的处女航(chǔ nǚ háng)①途中撞上冰山(iceberg), 2 小时 40 分钟后沉没。船上 2222 人中的 1516 人丧生(sàngshēng)。

沉没的故事: 泰坦尼克号上的 8 名华人

改编: 骆 西

原创: 黄 倩

泰坦尼克号沉没。*Titanic* sinking (1912), by Willy Stöwer, Magazine Die Gartenlaube. ⊘

泰坦尼克号的故事家喻户晓。在这艘豪华邮轮的三等(third class)舱里有 8 名华人乘客。在这次海难中，只有 6 名华人幸存，另外 2 名不幸遇难。为什么他们的故事却和泰坦尼克号的神话②一起沉入北大西洋(North Atlantic Ocean)冰冷的海底了呢？这 8 名华人的名字是：

Fang Lang 方荣森(Fong Long)32 岁，Lee Bing 李炳(Lee Ping)32 岁，Ah Lam 37 岁，Chang Chip 钟捷(Chong Chip)32 岁，Chong Foo(Chung Foo)32 岁，Lang Hee(Yum Hee)24 岁，Ling Lee 林利(遇难)，Len Lam(遇难)。

从泰坦尼克号发出的最后一艘救生艇。The last lifeboat successfully launched from the *Titanic* (1912). Courtesy of the Library of Congress.

他们都来自中国广东，本来在一艘往来于英国和中国的 蒸汽船 (steam ship)上工作。蒸汽船烧煤(coal)，这8名华人是船上的锅炉工(stoker)。1912年初，因为英国全国的煤矿工人(coal miner)罢工(strike)，所以蒸汽船没了煤烧，只能停运。这8名华人锅炉工也就失业了。这时，美国向他们打开了大门。这8名华人就买了三等舱的船票(15美元 - 40美元，相当于现在170美元 - 460美元)，登上了泰坦尼克号，投奔新雇主去了。

泰坦尼克号三等舱里有709名乘客，他们大多是想到美国或加拿大(Canada)寻梦的移民。在泰坦尼克号撞上冰山之后，冰水灌入(pour in)船舱。船员要做的第一件事是保证(ensure)头等舱和二等舱乘客的撤离(evacuation)。三等舱的乘客被要求留在船舱里。8名华人因为不太懂英语，出于求生本能(life instinct)，很快就开始自救。

6名华人幸存者中的5名跳上了救生艇(lifeboat)，还有一名叫方荣森的则把自己绑(tie up)在一块门板上。他被返回的14号救生艇发现。开始救生艇上的人还犹豫要不要救这个"日本人"，因为方荣森漂浮(float)在冰冷的海水中，脸朝下，好像已经死了。最后人们还是把他拉上了船。在众人的帮助下，他很快就醒了过来，开始说大家听不懂的话。不久，方荣森发现身边划船的人已经筋疲力尽，就推开划船的人，自己用力地划起来，直到所有人

安全到达了接应的船上。他的卖力^{mài lì}令之前不想救他的人很惭愧，并保证只要

有机会，还会救他！

沉船发生时，方荣森把自己绑在一块门板上在冰冷的海水中漂荡，绘画来自韩梅。
Fang Lang tying himself to a door panel and floating in the icy torrent, by Mei Han.

之后，这 6 名华人和泰坦尼克号上的其他 700 名幸存者被从纽约出发的

卡佩夏号^{kǎ pèi xià hào}(Carpathia)救起。船长决定带着这 706 名幸存者返回纽约。 经过三

天的航行，卡佩夏号在 1912 年 4 月 18 日晚上 9 点抵达了曼哈顿^{màn hā dùn}(Manhattan)。

这晚，天空下着冷雨，然而码头^{mǎ tóu}还是挤满了 4 万多迎接泰坦尼克号幸存者的

人，有乘客的家人，政府官员^{zhèng fǔ guānyuán}(government official)，医疗救护人员^{yī liáo jiù hù rén yuán}

(medical ambulance staff)，还有记者^{jì zhě}(reporter)。幸存者立刻受到了回家般

的待遇^{dài yù}(treatment)：有些被送去检查，有些住进了附近的酒店^{jiǔ diàn}(hotel)；即使

123

是船上三等舱的乘客也得到了慈善(charity)机构的帮助。然而，同样是死里

逃生，等待 6 名华人的却是被诽谤(defame)和被驱逐(deport)出境的命运。

　　中国人常说"大难不死必有后福"③。要知道，三等舱男乘客的 生 存率

只有七分之一。可是这 6 名华人躲过了大海难却没有躲过"排华法案"（即

《关于执行有关华人条约诸规定的法律》）。 因为早在 1882 年美国国会通过

的这项法案规定，所有的华工(Chinese laborer)都被禁止入境。6 名华人被

送上离自由女神像 300 米远的埃利斯岛(Ellis Island)④，停留一夜之后，第二

天就被送上雇佣他们的阿纳塔号(Annetta)货轮去了古巴(Cuba)。除此，还有

谣言(rumor)称这 6 名华人之所以能够活下来是因为偷偷躲在救生艇上。但是

当时每一艘救生艇都有持 枪 的(armed)船员把守(guard)，这种情况是不会发

生的。报纸上关于华人幸存者的报道则充满了侮辱性的(insulting)语言，称

他们为"苦力 (coolies) "、"黄皮肤的 中 国佬 (Yellow Chinks) "。

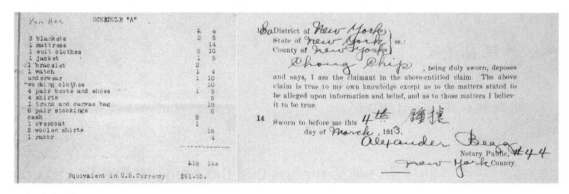

索赔文件。United States District Court, Southern District of New York. Courtesy of Qing
Huang.

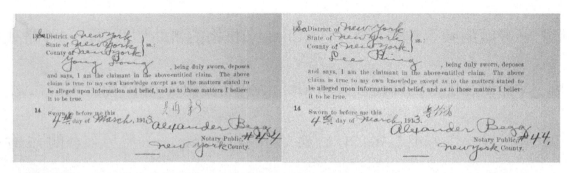

索赔文件。United States District Court, Southern District of New York. Courtesy of Qing Huang.

泰坦尼克号幸存者的故事被一遍又一遍地书写，拍成电影，而这 6 名华人的故事却在历史中销声匿迹。当泰坦尼克号的乘客向航运公司提起索赔(claim)时，至少 5 名泰坦尼克上的华人都获得了赔偿 (compensation)。6 名华人幸存者中的方荣森后来又回到美国生活。可是他们要么怕再次被驱逐，要么不愿意再提起那件令自己名誉(reputation)受损的事，所以泰坦尼克号上 8 个华人的故事也就渐渐没人知道了。

练 习

一、注解 Notes

① 处女航：maiden voyage.

② 泰坦尼克号的神话。神话 means that the name of the *Titanic* comes from Greek mythology. On the other hand, 神话 is also used to describe something which is too good to be true or to be surpassed. For example:马云(Jack Ma)的成功神话。

125

③ 大难不死必有后福：Those who survive a catastrophe are bound to have good fortune later on.

④ 埃利斯岛(Ellis Island)，in Upper New York Bay, was the gateway for over 12 million immigrants to the U.S. as the United States' busiest immigrant inspection station for over 60 years from 1892 until 1954.

二、生词 New Words

沉没	chén mò	sunken
家喻户晓	jiā yù hù xiǎo	to be known to every household
豪华	háo huá	luxury
邮轮	yóu lún	cruise/liner
幸存的	xìng cún de	to survive
遇难的	yù nàn de	to die in an accident
一艘	yì sōu	艘 is a measure word for ship 一艘船
罢工	bà gōng	to strike
失业	shī yè	to be unemployed
投奔	tóu bēn	to go to (a friend or a place) for shelter
雇主	gù zhǔ	employer
犹豫	yóu yù	to hesitate
筋疲力尽	jīn pí lì jìn	exhausted

接应	jiē yìng	to come to somebody's aid
卖力	mài lì	to do one's very best
惭愧	cán kuì	to be ashamed, 感到惭愧
死里逃生	sǐ lǐ táo shēng	to be saved from death
销声匿迹	xiāo sheng nì jì	vanished

三、阅读理解 Reading Comprehension

1. Where did the eight Chinese passengers work before boarding the *Titanic*?

A. Guangdong, China

B. New York, USA

C. Southampton, England

D. A steam ship

2. What happened to the eight Chinese passengers who were abroad the *Titanic*?

A. They met other immigrants who wanted to go to the US.

B. They were assigned a cabin in third class.

C. When the shipwreck occurred, they were not the first to be rescued.

D. All of the above.

3. What adjective best describes the people who did not want to save 方荣森 at first?

A. proud

B. sad

127

C. ashamed

D. affirmative

4. Which of the following statements is TRUE?

A. All eight Chinese passengers survived.

B. Five Chinese passengers survived.

C. 方荣森 was later rescued by a lifeboat.

D. 方荣森 didn't help other people on the lifeboat.

5. What happened to the *Titanic*'s six Chinese survivors when they arrived in New York?

A. They were heartily welcomed.

B. The newspapers reported their stories fairly.

C. Their claim for compensation was rejected.

D. They were deported the day after they arrived in New York.

Reference:

美华史记| 泰坦尼克号上的 8 名华人

https://mp.weixin.qq.com/s/FT3a1OyeacgvY-5F1X6f3g

BACKGROUND

The Titanic was a luxury English ocean liner that, at the time, was the world's largest ship and was considered by many as unsinkable. Tragically, the Titanic struck an iceberg during its maiden voyage from Southampton, England to New York City—within two hours of it striking the iceberg on April 14, 1912, the ship sank below the waves, killing 1,561 out of its 2,222 passengers.

Tales of the *Titanic*: The Eight Chinese Voyagers of the *Titanic*

Translated by Allan Zhao

The story of the *Titanic* is well known around the world. However, few know about the *Titanic*'s eight Chinese passengers. These passengers were part of the *Titanic*'s third class. Remarkably, six of the eight Chinese passengers would survive the tragedy that would soon follow. How did they escape the fate of their fellow passengers, and why did their story fade into the depths of the Atlantic?

The eight Chinese passengers were:

1.   Fang Lang (Fong Long) – 32
2.   Lee Bing (Lee Ping) – 32
3.   Ah Lam – 37
4.   Chang Chip (Chong Chip) – 32
5.   Chong Foo (Chung Foo) – 32

6.   Lang Hee (Yum Hee) – 24

7.   Ling Lee - Unknown[1]

8.   Len Lam – Unknown[1]

The eight Chinese passengers were from Guangdong and originally worked as stokers on steam ships between the United Kingdom and China. These workers would lose their job due to a coal strike at the beginning of 1912.[2] After losing their jobs, the Chinese workers, drawn to the idea of jobs and opportunity in the New World, aspired to immigrate to the United States; they bought third class tickets on the *Titanic* (the tickets costed fifteen to forty dollars, equivalent to 170 to 460 dollars today).

The *Titanic* had 709 third-class passengers, most of whom were aspiring immigrants to both the United States and Canada. When the *Titanic* struck the iceberg in the early morning, the icy water rushed into the ship's lower compartments. The crew, realizing the danger of the water, acted to ensure the safety of the first- and second-class passengers. They ordered the passengers to stay inside their own rooms—dooming most of the third-class passengers. The Chinese passengers, despite not knowing English, quickly recognized their own peril and acted to save themselves.

Out of the six Chinese survivors, five of them were able to jump onto lifeboats. The other survivor, Fang Lang, was able to survive by tying himself onto a door and floating away from the sinking vessel. Fang Lang was later pulled out of the water by the number 14 lifeboat[3]. The occupants of the lifeboat were initially hesitant to rescue the "Jap" man because Fang

---

[1] Ling Lee and Len Lam both died in the Titanic. Their ages are unknown.
[2] The national coal strike of 1912 was the first major English coal mine strike in modern history. The strike was resolved after 37 days, but the disruption to coal mining caused mass firings and delays in the train and shipping industries.
[3] Lifeboat 14 was commanded by Fifth Officer Harold Lowe. The passengers aboard the lifeboat eventually rescued around 25 survivors from the Titanic after the ship sank.

Lang was floating face down in the water, appearing to have already drowned. Eventually, the passengers agreed to pull Fang Lang out of the water, resuscitating him while in the lifeboat. Fang Lang did not understand English and nobody could understand what he was speaking. Despite this, he recognized the crew was tired from rowing the lifeboat. He took up the oars to the lifeboat and rowed until everybody was eventually rescued by the Carpathia, four hours later. His efforts embarrassed the people who had not been willing to save him, and they later said that they would save him again whenever they had the chance.

The captain of the Carpathia decided to send the six Chinese survivors, along with the 700 other survivors of the *Titanic*, to New York. After three days of sailing, the Carpathia arrived at Manhattan at 9 pm on April 18, 1912. Over forty thousand people braved the cold and rainy weather in the evening to welcome the survivors of the *Titanic*. Some of these were family members of the passengers, others were government officials, reporters or medical workers. Some of the survivors were sent to hospitals while others were sent to local hotels. Even third-class passengers received kind charity from the locals. However, the six Chinese survivors did not receive the same welcome; they were ridiculed by locals for surviving while others perished in the ocean and later deported.

Chinese people often say that those who survive a catastrophe are bound to have good fortune later on. However, the survivors did not escape the Chinese Exclusion Act. The six survivors were deported because the 1882 Chinese Exclusion Act banned Chinese laborers from entering the country. The six survivors were sent to Ellis Island, only 300 meters away from the Statue of Liberty. After staying overnight, they were sent by the Annetta freighter to Cuba. After their deportation, rumors abounded that the

Chinese passengers disguised themselves or hid under the seats of the lifeboat to survive.[4] The newspapers called the Chinese "coolies" and "chinks" and dismissed claims that any Chinese survived the sinking as insulting.

Later, the passengers of the *Titanic* sued the operator of the *Titanic*. At least five Chinese survivors on the *Titanic* have received compensation. Fang Lang was the sole Chinese survivor that eventually made his way to the United States, but fearing deportation and harm to his reputation, he refused to tell the story, eventually leading to the Chinese survivors' story fading to obscurity. The story of the *Titanic* has been told many times; it has even been made into an Academy Award winning movie. However, one of its most interesting stories has faded to obscurity, hidden along with the remains of the *Titanic*, in the depths of the ocean.

---

[4] These rumors were later proven false by eyewitness testimony since all of the lifeboats had armed guards in front, making it impossible for passengers to be sneak into the lifeboats before they were launched by the crew

美国第一位华裔律师洪耀宗

改编: 潘秋辰

原创: 周洁

1898 年 5 月 4 日，旧金山修筑中央铁路华工中的一户洪姓家庭，诞生了一名男孩，取名"耀宗"，意为光 宗耀祖。

5 岁时，洪耀宗的父亲去世了，从此全家依靠不懂英文的母亲在卷烟厂做工来维持生计。母亲每星期给他 1 分钱，他用这 1 分钱在华人点心铺买来一大盒油酥蛋糕的渣沫，足够兄弟姐妹们享用好几天。

有一天，一位叔叔逗弄年幼的耀宗，不小心失手，造成他脊椎受伤，致使他的身高发育受到影响。小耀宗并没有因此失去开朗的天性，依旧积极认真学习语言，时常帮助母亲与外界沟通。稍长大一些，他跟小伙伴们设计了英语会话书来教习其他华人，比如：买东西、问路、搭 乘公交车等基本会话。到高中时期，洪耀宗因其突出的英文能力，担任当地移民局翻译，从翻译工作中，他了解到华人被移民局刁难盘问的许多问题。

1920 年，22 岁的洪耀宗收到了南加州大学法学院的录取通知书。他成为该院录取的第一位华裔学生，也是最穷的一位学生。他买不起教科书，但是同学们看他勤奋好学，便轮流借书给他用。1922 年，洪耀宗顺利通过加州律师资格考试，成为该州历史上第一位华裔执业律师。

那个时代，很多在美国打拼的华人男子一般都选择回国成婚，婚后再独自回到美国继续做工。因此申请家庭团聚便成为这些没有专业法律知识的华工的最大梦想。为了让更多同胞骨肉团聚，洪耀宗以自己的法律知识，陆续为约 7300 名华人家属取得了合法移民资格。在这些人中，就有美国历史上第一位华裔联邦大法官刘成威的父亲，他在洪耀宗的帮助下得以在美国洛杉矶定居，并于 1939 年和全家团聚。为此刘大法官的父亲始终教导刘成威要以洪律师为榜样，为华裔争取合法权益。

华裔美国公民联盟代表团出席众议院移民和归化问题听证会。Chinese American Citizens Alliance delegation to hearings before the House of Representatives Committee on Immigration and Naturalization. Y. C. Hong is the second person from the right on the front row. Kenneth Y. Fung is the first person from the right on the second row. Henry Lowe is the first person from the left in the second row (1928). The Huntington Library, Art Collections, and Botanical Gardens.

洪耀宗在长期受理华裔移民案件的过程中，发现最大的阻碍即为1882年5 月 6 日美国国会通过的第一个限禁外来移民的法案《关于执行有关华人条约诸规定的法律》，即"排华法案"。当时该法案已历经数次延长，被彻底取消了时限，也就意味着对华人的歧视将永远存在。

早期美国允许一些中国移民，如商人和公民的配偶进入美国，后来这项规定也被取缔了（qǔ dì）。移民局甚至怀疑华人伪造亲属甚至血缘关系，从洛杉矶和旧金山入境的中国人经常要被盘问 100 至 400 多个涉及家族史的问题，并接受严格的体检。

为了让那些妻儿尚在中国大陆的华人得以与家人团聚，洪耀宗开始联合一些社会活动家积极奔走呼告（bēn zǒu hū gào）。他向民选议员申诉：在美国做工的中国男子需要结婚成家，但并不是每个人都愿意与不同族裔通婚，选择自己的配偶是他们的权利。

无数事实让洪耀宗认识到必须纠正不公正的"排华法案"。早在 1928 年，30 岁的洪耀宗出席华盛顿关于美国移民和归化问题听证会时，便以条理清晰（tiáo lǐ qīng xī）、逻辑性强的口才和专业法律素养，向国会议员痛陈了"排华法案"的流弊（liú bì），以及带给整个族裔的歧视和伤害。洪耀宗作为一名远近闻名的华裔大律师，仍然需要随身携带有照片的身份证书，这种证书是许多华裔美国人为防止被驱逐出境而必须随身携带的。

在推动废除"排华法案"的过程中，恰逢洛杉矶兴建联合车站，规划选址在唐人街上，洪耀宗藉此契机（jiè cǐ qì jī），积极联合各华商，带动旧唐人街改造，并亲自上阵设计规划新唐人街。为此他专门学习了建筑学，亲手绘制图纸，指导施工。1938 年，洛杉矶市中心新唐人街落成了，这是美国第一个由华裔美国人规划设计的文化商务中心，一改往日贫民窟乱象，充分展示中国文化风貌，倡导各族裔移民跨越种族界限相互接纳支持。

迫于种种情势，1943 年 12 月 17 日，美国国会通过了《麦格努森法案》，亦称"排华法案废除案"，但实际上，直到 1965 年，移民改革法才终结了单独基于国籍或种族所设的限制法令。

洪耀宗和家人。Christmas portrait of the Hong Family (1960s). The Huntington Library, Art Collections, and Botanical Gardens.

洪耀宗自幼虽身有缺陷，但热爱运动，乐观向上，他本人也成为两个儿子成长的最佳表率，其一子成为律师，另一子成为建筑师。南加州大学法学院为表彰洪耀宗的贡献，创立了两个以他的名字命名的奖学金。洪耀宗于 1977 年 11 月去世，享年 79 岁。

今天，亨廷顿图书馆还挂有洪耀宗的名言："只要还存在一些我们认为从政治上、经济上或社会上仍不能接受的东西，那么对所有美国人来说，就仍存在危险"。

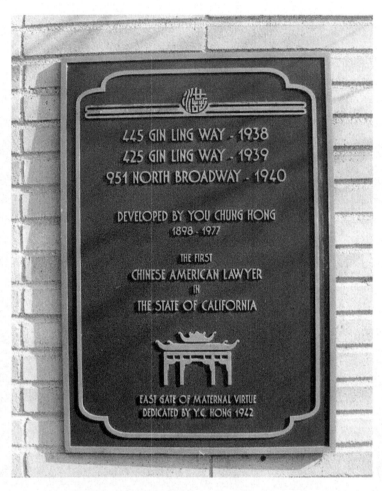

在洛杉矶新的唐人街的洪耀宗的纪念圖。Memorial plaque to You Chung Hong, California lawyer, in Los Angeles New Chinatown (2012). Photo by George Garrigues, GeorgeLouis at English Wikipedia (CC-BY-SA，3.0).

※本课需要积累的词汇：

光宗耀祖：glorify one's ancestors 或 bring honor to one's ancestors

维持生计：to maintain livelihoods

逗弄：to tease　　　　　　脊椎：spine

开朗：cheerful   盘问：cross-examination

刁难：to create difficulties

打拼：to fight   骨肉团聚：family reunion

权益：equity   阻碍：obstruction

歧视：discrimination   取缔：to ban

奔走呼告：to run and call   荒唐行径：absurd acts

驱逐出境：deportation   痛陈：to state with profound grief

流弊：disadvantages   契机：opportunity

乱象：chaotic phenomena

练 习

一、生词 **New Words**：根据拼音写出文中的词语。

guāng zōng yào zǔ	光宗耀祖	dòu nòng	_____
wéi chí shēng jì	_____	jǐ zhuī	_____
kāi lǎng	_____	diāo nàn	_____
pán wèn	_____	dǎ pīn	_____
gǔ ròu tuán jù	_____	zǔ ài	_____
quán yì	_____	qí shì	_____
luàn xiàng	_____	qì jī	_____
bēn zǒu hū gào	_____	qǔ dì	_____
qū zhú chū jìng	_____	liú bì	_____
huāng táng xíng jìng	_____	tòng chén	_____

二、阅读理解 **Reading Comprehension**

1．What is the Chinese meaning of the name "耀宗"?

A. Highly qualified people.

B. The ancestors were the chief officials.

C. An elderly father.

D. To glorify ancestors.

2. Which of the following statements is correct?

A. Hong Yaozong was the first Chinese judge in American history.

B. Hong Yaozong was very short because he contracted as a child.

C. During the Chinese Exclusion Act, the Immigration Bureau generally asked Chinese immigrants around 10 questions when they entered the United States.

D. The New Chinatown (built in 1938) in downtown Los Angeles was designed by Hong Yaozong.

3．Which university law school created two scholarships under You Chung's name to honor his contributions?

A. Harvard University

B. Yale University

C. University of Southern California

D. Stanford University

4．This quote is in the last paragraph of the article：洪耀宗的名言："只要还存在一些我们认为从政治上、经济上或社会上仍不能接受的东西，那么对所有美国人来说，就仍存在危险" What does it mean?

A. The United States is a dangerous country.

B. As long as Chinese Americans face discrimination at the hands of Americans, this country will not be truly free.

C. Chinese do not understand politics and economy, so they are dangerous.

D. As long as there are some of us considered still unacceptable politically, economically or socially, it remains a dangerous situation for all Americans.

三、请分组进行下列对话训练

人物角色 A：星宇(男)；

人物角色 B：琪琪(女)。

星宇：我长大了想当一名律师，你呢？琪琪。

琪琪：我也想当一名律师，收入高，又稳定，对我来说这是一份称心如意的工作。

星宇：如果你遇到了不平等的法律条款，你会像洪耀宗律师那样跳出来为民众打官司吗？

琪琪：将来，作为一个女性律师，我不想去参与太多抛头露面的活动，像经济赔偿律师就比较好，难度也没有这么大。

星宇：但是我是一名男子汉，我觉得'天下兴亡，匹夫有责'，我一定会像洪耀宗律师那样，为所有民众的民主、平等而努力的。

琪琪：你真有志向，我要向你学习。

星宇：其实，有很多著名的女律师也是为人权而战的，她们头脑敏捷，知识丰富，逻辑性强。

琪琪：我吧，心里也有这样的想法，只是对自己没有信心……

星宇：没有关系，世上无难事，只怕有心人，自信心是一点一点培养起来的，我们大家可以互相鼓励，给对方以信心和力量。

琪琪：好呀，以后你要多鼓励我，让我就有更多的勇气锻炼自己。

星宇：没问题，一言为定。

琪琪：那让我们再接再厉吧！

四、写作训练：请你从上面对话训练里出现的成语中挑选三个，写一段自己的话。

抛头露面：to show up

称心如意：to be satisfied

天下兴亡，匹夫有责：The rise and fall of the nation, everyone is responsible.

世上无难事，只怕有心人：Nothing in the world is unachievable for one who sets his mind to it.

一言为定：It's agreed. A promise is a promise.

再接再厉：to make persistent efforts

_____

_____

_____

_____

_____

_____

Reference：

美华史记|华裔人物：加州华裔律师破冰第一人洪耀宗

https://mp.weixin.qq.com/s/zYTW8-XHDWc89_ggWBT-Mg

The First Chinese American Lawyer: You Chung Hong

Translated by Rebecca Kuang

On 4 May 1898, a baby boy was born to the Hong family, which worked in railroad construction in San Francisco. He was named Yaozong (You Chung). This name expressed the wish that he would bring honor to his ancestors.

You Chung's father passed away when he was five years old. From then on, the entire family depended on You Chung's mother, a cigarette factory worker who couldn't speak English, for their livelihoods. Every week, You Chung's mother would give him a penny, which he used to buy a big box of cake crumbs from a Chinese dim sum shop. This was enough to feed him and his siblings for several days.

One day, You Chung accidentally sustained a spinal injury while playing with an uncle. Although this stunted his growth, little You Chung didn't lose his carefree and cheerful nature. Just as before, he earnestly studied languages, frequently helping his mother to communicate with outsiders. Once he was a bit older, he and some of his friends designed some conversation books to help other Chinese Americans practice their English. Example topics included going shopping, asking for directions, riding public transportation, and other fundamental subjects of conversation. When You Chung was in high school, he worked as a translator for the local immigration office because of his excellent English. In the course of his translation work, You Chung learned about many difficult questions that immigrants were asked during interrogations by the immigration office.

In 1920, the 22-year old You Chung was admitted to the University of Southern California Law School. He was the law school's first Chinese American student, as well as the poorest student in his class. He couldn't afford his textbooks, but his classmates noticed his diligence and eagerness to learn, and so took turns lending their books to him. In 1922, You Chung easily passed the California bar exam and became the very first Chinese American lawyer in California's history.

During that era, many working Chinese men chose to return to China to marry and then return alone to the United States after marriage to continue working. Therefore, these Chinese workers, who had no legal expertise, dreamed of applying for immigration papers to reunite their families. In order to help more of his countrymen reunite with their relatives, You Chung used his legal expertise to help about 7,300 families obtain the proper immigration papers. Among these immigrants was the father of Ronald S.W. Lew (Liu Chengwei), who settled in Los Angeles through You Chung's efforts and was reunited with his family in 1939. As a result, Lew's father always taught him to follow Hong's example and to fight for the legal rights of Chinese Americans.

Over a long career of handling Chinese immigration cases, Hong learned that the biggest obstacle to Chinese immigrants was an act that the United States Congress had passed on 6 May 1882, which was the first law to restrict the immigration of foreign nationals: "An Act to Execute Certain Treaty Stipulations Relating to the Chinese." This law was more popularly known as the "Chinese Exclusion Act." After several extensions, the act's time limits had been entirely abolished, which implied that discrimination against the Chinese might continue forever.

Initially the United States had permitted some Chinese immigrants such as businessmen and the spouses of citizens to enter the country. But later, this provision was also curtailed. The immigration office was so suspicious that Chinese immigrants were faking kinship relations that immigrants at Los Angeles and San Francisco often had to undergo interrogations of 100 to 400 questions about their families, as well as rigorous medical examinations.

In order to help Chinese men to reunite with their wives and children still in mainland China, You Chung began to organize some social activists to ardently advocate for Chinese rights. He filed a complaint to elected lawmakers, arguing that Chinese workers in the United States needed to be able to marry and start a family. Not everyone was willing to enter interracial relationships, but everyone ought to have the right to choose their own spouse.

Countless cases made You Chung realize that the unjust Chinese Exclusion Act had to be revised. As early as 1928, the thirty-year-old Hong attended a Congressional hearing on the US immigration and naturalization issue in Washington. Using both his legal expertise and clear, logical diction, he told Congress of the abuses of the Chinese Exclusion Act, as well as how it harmed and discriminated against an entire race. Even though You Chung was a well-known Chinese American lawyer, he still had to carry photographic identity on his person wherever he went. Many Chinese Americans had to carry around identification in order to avoid deportation.

The process of the repeal of the Chinese Exclusion Act coincided with the construction of a new Union Station in Los Angeles, which was planned to be built in Chinatown. You Chung seized this opportunity to organize Chinese businessmen and spur the transformation of the old Chinatown. He personally designed and planned the new Chinatown. He learned architecture just for this project. He drew maps by hand and directed construction. The new Chinatown in the heart of Los Angeles was built in 1938. This was the first cultural and commercial center in America that was planned and designed by a Chinese American. It transformed the mess of the slum housing of the past and put the features of Chinese culture on full display. It encouraged immigrants of different ethnicities to cross racial boundaries and mutually accept and support each other.

On 17 December 1943, under a number of circumstantial pressures, the United States Congress passed the Magnuson Act, also known as the Chinese Exclusion Repeal Act. However, in reality, immigration law did not change to end the practice of restricting immigration based solely on race or nationality until 1965.

Although You Chung had suffered a growth-stunting injury as a child, he loved exercise, and he was an excellent model of growth to his two sons. One became a lawyer, and one became an architect. The University of Southern California Law School created two scholarships under You Chung's name to honor his contributions. You Chung died at age 79 in 1977.

Today, a quote by You Chung Hong is displayed on a panel in the Huntington Library: "As long as there are some of us considered still unacceptable politically, economically or socially, it remains a dangerous situation for all Americans."

诗歌欣赏：萨凡纳的女诗人西格

Gerald Chan Sieg, the Poetess of Savannah

改编：骆 西

原创：张为华

乔治亚萨凡纳夜晚鸟瞰。Evening rooftop view of Savannah, Georgia (2014). Photo by RCraig09 (CC-BY-SA，3.0).

西格(Gerald Chan Sieg，1909 年 10 月 1 日-2005 年 6 月 30 日)出生于萨凡纳的①首个华人家庭。从小深受东西方文化的影响，西格的诗歌生动地反映了早期华人在美国南方的生活。在这篇文章中，同学们可以发现华人的足迹遍美国，华人不光可以修铁路，也可以用优美的诗歌来记录生活。

Gerald Chan Sieg (October 1, 1909 - June 30, 2005) was born to the first Chinese family in Savannah. Since her childhood, she was deeply influenced by both Western and Eastern influences. Sieg's poems vividly reflected the lives of the early Chinese in the American south. In this article, students will discover the footprints of Chinese people all over America. The Chinese were not just capable of building railroads; they could also employ graceful poetry to record their lives.

西格画像。绘画来自韩梅。Portrait of Gerald Chan Sieg by Mei Han.

下面这首《伤心的淑女》是西格 19 岁时第一次发表的诗歌，并在当地
的诗歌比赛中获奖。

《伤心的淑女》

东方花园，睡莲浮动，

淑女端坐，身着绣花衣，小脚绣红鞋，

珠玉满她手，珠玉满她头。

花影月下，歌谣轻唱，手指拨动，琵琶呜咽：

"小宝贝比蜜还甜，

多可爱，

小宝贝不在我身边……

多孤单，

小宝贝去了天边，永眠在花仙的冷臂弯，

多悲伤。"

东方花园，睡莲浮动，

伤心淑女，歌谣轻唱，

泪水涟涟，身着绣花衣，小脚绣红鞋

珠玉满她手，珠玉满她头。

The following poem "The Sad Lady" was Sieg's first published poem. It was written when Sieg was only nineteen years old and won a local poetry competition.

The Sad Lady

In an Eastern garden

Where the water lilies float

Sits the fair lady

In a jade-embroidered coat:

And tiny shoes of red,

Jewels on her fingers,

And jewels on her head.

This is the song she sings,

While the moonlit flowers sway

To the sobbing of the lute,

Which her fingers ever play:

"Sweeter than honey made by the bee,

Pretty one.

Little Pearl-boy was stolen from me . . .

I'm alone.

Little Pearl-boy is so far away.

He's asleep

In the cold arms of the flower fay . . .

And I weep."

So the sad lady sings

Where the water lilies float,

And in her eyes are tears,

Though she wears a 'broidered coat,

A jade-embroidered coat,

And tiny shoes of red,

Jewels on her fingers,

And jewels on her head.

西格的另一首诗《洗衣工》发表于 1934 年。诗里描写的内容可能跟她父亲早期从事的洗衣业有关，表现了早期华人移民的孤独。

《洗衣工》

假如我还能再听到一次，黑翅雀穿过稻田翠竹的召唤，
（hēi chì）

假如我还能再看见一次，直立于水草中的鹳雀鸟，
（guànquèniǎo）

假如我还能再摸到一次，她那藏在红袖里，纤细柔软的手指，
（xiān xì）

哦，神啊，我将心甘情愿地熨衣到永远。
（yùn）

Another poem by Sieg, "Laundryman", was published in 1934. The poem describes the poet's early experiences in the laundry industry with her father and illustrates the loneliness of early Chinese immigrants.

Laundryman

If I could hear once more

The call of dark winged birds across the fields

Of rice and slim young bamboo,

If I could see once more

A crane with yellow legs so straight

Among cool water grasses,

If I could touch again

Her hands whose fingers in the sleeve of scarlet

Are softly curled and gentle,

My soul would be content,

O gods,

To iron away eternity.

虽然西格从来没有去过中国，可是在诗歌《中国娃娃》中，她想象了一群快乐的中国儿童。

《中国娃娃》

三个小男孩、一个小女孩, 珠江②岸边一栋房。

一个小女孩、三个小男孩, 玩具件件棒。

gāoqiāo
高跷踩得好, 望过家中墙。

táng
小船塘中游, 荷叶绿又凉。

huàng
金鱼水中摆, 晃来又晃去。

猴子绳上爬，翠鸟把歌唱。
cuì niǎo

爆竹红又亮，一炮冲天上。
bào zhú pào

啊，一个小女孩 三个小男孩，玩具件件棒！

<u>Although Sieg never visited China, her poem "The Chinese Children"</u>
<u>imagines a group of happy Chinese children.</u>

The Chinese Children

Three small boys and one small girl

lived in a house on the River Pearl.

One small girl and three small boys

that had such very charming toys.

Stilts on which they walked so tall

that they could see above the wall.

A little junk to sail the pool

where lily leaves lay green and cool,

And where the golden fins below

went slowly gleamming to and fro.

A monkey climbing on a string

a jeweled bird that used to sing.

153

Some firecrackers red and bright
and rockets shooting out of sight.

Oh, what fascinating toys
for one small girl and three small boys!

练 习

一、注解 NOTE

① 萨凡纳(Savannah)建于 1733 年，是美国佐治亚州最古老的城市。在文学作品中萨凡纳是《金银岛》(Treasure Island)海盗 船 长 (pirate captain)^{hǎi dàochuánzhǎng}弗林特醉死的地方。死前他把金银岛的地图交给了比利·彭斯(Billy Bones)。在另一部巨著《飘》(Gone with the wind)中，萨凡纳是斯嘉丽·奥哈拉(Scarlett O'Hara)眼中的一位老祖母。除此，萨凡纳还是个特别的花园城市，城市里每百米就有一座花园。据说修建这些花园的目的是为了让更多的人步行，使时间慢下来。

尤金塔尔马奇纪念大桥。骆西拍摄。Eugene Talmadge Memorial Bridge (2018). Photo by Xi Luo.

154

② 珠江(Pearl river)是中国第二大河流。在这首诗里指中国的广东地区。

二、延伸思考 Extension Thinking

《静夜思》

李白(唐代)

窗前明月光（guāng），

疑是地上霜（shuāng）。

举头望明月，

低头思故乡（xiāng）。

A rhyme is a repetition of similar sounds in the final stressed syllables of two or more words. Like "光"、"霜"、"乡" in Li Bai's 《静夜思》。 Can you create a rhyming poem in Chinese?

_____

_____

_____

_____

_____

Reference:

美华史记 | 西格：洗衣工的女儿, 萨凡纳的诗人
https://mp.weixin.qq.com/s/6dtRES6pcNdHEVlgt_bLWg

林凯蒂抗争种族隔离的故事

改编：潘秋辰

原创：水 文

1927 年 10 月，美国最高法院受理了密西西比州林凯蒂(Katherine Lum)一家状告学区董事会一案。

凯蒂是凯瑟琳的昵称，她小时候是个孤儿，被一家富有的黄姓商人家庭收养。1912 年她年满 18 岁后，认识了在杂货店工作的林江功(Jeu Gong Lum，音译)。第二年，凯蒂和林江功喜结连理，婚后在小镇伯努瓦(Benoit)开了一家小店，开始了新生活。1914 年，他们的第一个孩子诞生了，取名波妲(Berta)；随后，女儿玛莎(Martha)和儿子毕斯可(Biscoe)相继出生。

凯蒂自幼在基督徒家庭长大，英语流利，婚后每星期日依然去白人教会做礼拜。为了让儿女接受良好的教育，他们夫妻俩搬到玫瑰谷(Rosedale)开了新店。1924 年秋季，这两个分别为三、四年级的小姑娘在开学这天进入了玫瑰谷镇学校——一所三角洲地区教学水平一流的学校。

中午时分，两个女儿回来了。新上任的校长告诉她们：玫瑰谷学校董事会不接受华人孩子到这所白人学校上学。

玫瑰谷学校。水文拍摄。Rosedale Consolidated School. Photo by Shuiwen (2018).

　　这对凯蒂来说是当头一棒。她听说过前州长额尔·布鲁尔(Earl Brewer)律师曾帮助过华人，夫妇俩决定请他打官司，状告校董(L. C. Brown, Greek. P. Rice 以及 Henry McGowen 等人)。

玫瑰谷学校铭牌，1924 年 McGowen 仍然担任校董。水文拍摄。Commemorative Plaque of Rosedale Consolidated School. Photo by Shuiwen (2018).

布鲁尔律师向法庭陈述：玛莎是一个出生在密西西比州的 9 岁女孩，一个优秀的小学生。仅仅因为种族原因就被赶出了白人学校，这违背了宪法第十四修正案。① 同时，密西西比州法律规定，不得禁止 5 到 18 岁少年儿童上学。那么，玛莎上学的权利同样应该得到州法的保护。

校董会提出抗辩(kàngbiàn)：不准玛莎上这个学校的根据是密西西比州宪法第 207 条：学校实行白人与黑人隔离(gé lí)的制度，因为玛莎是"蒙古或黄色人种"，所以她只能上"有色人种"的学校。

1924 年 11 月 5 日巡回法庭法官威廉·奥尔康(ào ěr kāng)(William Alcorn)驳回抗辩，命令玫瑰谷镇学校接受玛莎姐妹回去上学。

校董会以及他们背后强大的种族隔绝势力并未就此罢休。12 月 15 日，校董会向州最高法院提出上诉，州司法总长担任了校董会的头牌律师。当时没有其他华人加入凯蒂一家的行动，他们孤军奋战(gū jūn fèn zhàn)，但仍决定继续抗争下去。

作为州法院最重要的案子开庭了，校董会律师埃尔默·克林顿·沙珀(Elmer Clinton Sharp)陈述：密西西比州的政策从来都是白人学校只面向白人孩子。玛莎和其他所有的华人儿童都应该归类为"尼格罗(Negros)"，而该州已经"创造"了种族隔离制度以保护白人利益，就没有必要考虑任何联邦宪法。

布鲁尔指出当 1890 年种族隔离制度建立时，密西西比州只有黑人和白人，玛莎是本州儿童，不管肤色如何，她享有在本州公立学校接受教育的权利。但是，州最高法院裁定：玛莎不是白人，所以她不能进入玫瑰谷镇的白人学校。

凯蒂一家输了，她决定送孩子到没有种族隔离制度的密执安州去上学。1925 年 5 月，11 岁的波姐带着 10 岁的妹妹和 6 岁的弟弟踏上了北去的火车，坐在标注"有色人种"的车厢里。学校里所有非白人族裔的孩子都被这样不公平地对待，小姐妹受伤的心灵总算得了一丝抚慰。

这时，一位华人商人(J. K. Young)向凯蒂一家伸出了援手。他的祖先早年来到三角洲，在孟菲斯以南的图尼卡(Tunika)开杂货店。他一直密切注视着案情发展，当布鲁尔律师败诉后，他自告奋勇，以凯蒂一家法律代理人身份给联邦最高法院写信，要求提供以前的庭审文件并要求此案排入开庭期。

1927 年 11 月 21 日，最高法院大法官威廉·塔夫茨(William Taft)发布了九位法官一致通过的判决。他们认为本案的关键问题是：出生在美国的中国血统儿童只能上"接受有棕色、黄色或黑色人种的孩子"的学校是否剥夺了对她的平等保护。但最终的判决书还是支持了种族隔离政策。

几天之内，全国各主要报纸都登载了此案的结果，这意味着三角洲的华人代表竭尽全力的抗争失败了。

凯蒂继续为孩子们的教育寻找出路。终于，她在密西西比河对岸阿肯色州的伊蕾因(Elaine)找到一所愿意接受华人孩子的白人学校。尽管校舍陈旧，师资条件差，凯蒂一家还是离开玫瑰谷，搬到学校附近开了个小小的杂货店。因为那时华人不得拥有不动产，一家人十几年的奋斗就归了零，重新回到贫穷状态。而且杂货店生意维持不了生计，凯蒂每天一大早起来烘焙面包以补贴家用，但她心中仍抱着一线希望。

1933 年波妲和玛莎高中毕业，玛莎进入阿肯色州州立大学师范专业学习。二战开始后，姐妹俩还到加州长滩的兵工厂里 装 配轰炸机。1940 年弟弟参军，后被派遣到中国云南的美军战地医院工作。

在反对种族歧视、捍卫宪法赋予的平等权利的长期斗争中，凯蒂全家始终没有放弃。直到 1954 年的布朗诉托皮卡教育局案，最高法院裁定：种族隔离这种制度本身就违背了宪法。

这一裁定也否决了 1927 年建立在种族隔离合法基础上对凯蒂一家的判决。从此，种族主义的藩篱终于得以拆除。

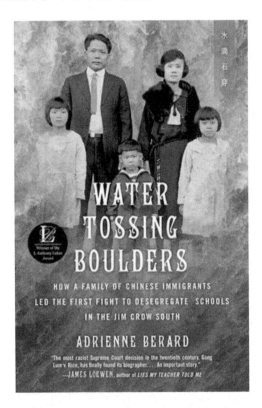

凯蒂一家。The Lum family. "Water Tossing Boulders: How a Family of Chinese Immigrants Led the Fight to Desegregate Schools in the Jim Crow South". Copyright © 2016 by Adrienne Berard. Reprinted with permission from Beacon Press, Boston, Massachusetts.

练 习

一、注解 NOTES

① 1868 年 7 月 9 日通过的宪法第十四修正案：所有在合众国出生或者归化合众国并受其司法管辖的人，都是合众国的，也是他们所居住州的公民。任何一州都不得制定或实施法律限制合众国公民的特权或豁免权，不得拒绝给任何人以平等法律保护。

二、生词 New Words：请写出正确的拼音。

昵称 nickname	_____	生计 livelihood	_____
禁止 to forbid	_____	烘焙 to bake	_____
驳回 to reject	_____	派遣 to send	_____
抚慰 to comfort	_____	藩篱 fence	_____

昵称　nickname　_____　生计　livelihood　_____

禁止　to forbid　_____　烘焙　to bake　_____

驳回　to reject　_____　派遣　to send　_____

抚慰　to comfort　_____　藩篱　fence　_____

竭尽全力　　　to do your best　_____

自告奋勇　　　to volunteer　_____

孤军奋战　　　to fight alone　_____

当头一棒(震惊)　a head-on blow, to get shocked　_____

三、练习与运用 Drills and Practice：请注意文中有以下字词的句子，并用该字词造一个句子。

(一) 被、把、将

她小时候是个孤儿，被一家富有的黄姓商人家庭收养。

_____

她小时候是个孤儿，一家富有的黄姓商人家庭把(将)她收养。

161

由于她是华人后代就被赶出了白人学校，这违背了宪法第十四修正案。

好在学校里所有非白人族裔的孩子都被这样不公平地对待，小姐妹受伤的心灵总算得了一丝抚慰。

1940 年弟弟参军，后被派遣到中国云南的美军战地医院工作。

(二) 和、以及

凯蒂和林江功喜结连理。

女儿玛莎(Martha)和儿子毕斯可(Biscoe)相继出生。

玛莎和其他所有的华人儿童都应该归类为"尼格罗"。

当 1890 年种族隔离制度建立时，密西西比州只有黑人和白人。

11 岁的波妲带着 10 岁的妹妹和 6 岁的弟弟踏上了北去的火车。

受理了林凯蒂一家状告学区董事会，以及当地最高法院的案子。

_____

校董会以及他们背后强大的种族隔绝势力并未就此罢休。

_____

(三) 就

由于她是华人后代就被赶出了白人学校，这违背了宪法第十四修正案。

_____

校董会以及他们背后强大的种族隔绝势力并未就此罢休。

_____

该州已经"创造"了种族隔离制度以保护白人利益，就没有必要考虑任何联邦宪法。

_____

种族隔离这种制度本身就违背了宪法。

_____

四、阅读理解 Reading Comprehension

1. Why did the Lums' move to Rosedale to open a new grocery store？

A. Because there were so many people, it was easy to do business and make more money.

B. Because they were not welcomed, they could not stay in Benoit any longer.

C. Because they wanted their children to get a good education.

D. Because they wanted to move closer to the school their children were admitted in.

2. How many years did it take for schools to finally be desegregated?
    A. 54   B. 27
    C. 20   D. 10

3. Under Mississippi law, at what ages should children attend school?
    A. 7 to 16   B. 5 to 18
    C. 7 to 18   D. 7 to 14

4. Why did the Lums hire former governor Earl Brewer to represent them?

A. The judge dared not offend him because he was a local celebrity.

B. Because he was a friend of the Lums.

C. Because he was a free, warm-hearted lawyer.

D. Because he even helped Chinese people.

五、判断正误，请在正确的句子前面写"T"，错误的句子前面写"F"

Please write "T" before correct sentences and "F" before incorrect sentences：

(　　) 1. The Lums sued the school board because the headmaster beat and cursed Lums' children.

(　　) 2. The Lums sued the school board and the local court in order to draw public attention.

(　　) 3. The Lums received assistance from many Chinese during the long legal process.

(　　) 4. The Lums moved many times for the children's schooling.

六、请你模仿文中的人物把下面这场辩论继续下去……(**Please continue this debate by acting the characters in the passage...**)。

人物 1：林凯蒂(**Katherine Lum**)

人物 2：林家律师(**Lum's lawyer**)

人物 3：法官(**the judge**)

人物 4：校董(**the school board**)

人物 5：校董律师(**the school board's lawyer**)

人物 6：玛莎(**Martha**)

林家律师： 法官先生，林凯蒂夫妇在这里十多年来遵纪守法，他们经营杂货铺诚实可靠，深得居民喜爱。他们的三个孩子都出生在这里，为什么不能像所有公民一样享有上学的权利呢？

玛莎： 我非常热爱学习，我是个品学兼优的好学生。

校董： 但是我们这里从很早的时候就有州法律将黑人和白人隔离开来，白人学校从来不接收有色人种子弟的。

林凯蒂： 政府为有色人种开办的学校，又差又落后，大家都是纳税人，为什么这么不公平呢？

校董律师： 本州既然有针对黑人和白人的种族隔离法，那么有色人种就应当与黑人一样被隔离，以此捍卫白人的权利。

法官： 那么，1868 年 7 月 9 日通过的宪法第十四修正案是这样说的：所有在合众国出生或者归化合众国并受其司法管辖的人，都是合众国的也是他们所居住州的公民。任何一州都不得制定或实施法律限制合众国公民的特权或豁免权，不得拒绝给任何人以平等的法律保护。

……

……

七、写作训练 Writing Practice： 请你用文中出现的下列成语，写一段自己的话。

当头一棒：to get shocked　　　　孤军奋战：to fight alone

166

自告奋勇：to volunteer   竭尽全力：to do your best

_____

_____

_____

_____

_____

_____

_____

_____

_____

_____

_____

References：
1. 华裔人物：南国铁娘子，风雨木兰花——林凯蒂挺身而出抗争种族隔离的故事
https://mp.weixin.qq.com/s/5DYrOpg1vFMdG4wqhbOW3g
2. Water Tossing Boulders: How a Family of Chinese Immigrants Led the First Fight to Desegregate Schools in the Jim Crow South by Adrienne Berard. Beacon Press.

The Story of Kate Lum's Fight Against Racial Segregation

Translated by Rebecca Kuang

In October 1927, the Supreme Court of the United States took up the case of the Lum family's suit against the Mississippi school board of trustees.

"Kate" was Katherine Lum's nickname. She was orphaned at a young age and subsequently adopted into the wealthy Wong family. When she turned eighteen in 1912, she met Jeu Gong Lum, who worked at a grocery store. Kate and Jeu Gong were married the next year. They opened a small store in a little town called Benoit and began their new lives.

Kate, who had grown up in a Christian household, spoke fluent English. After she was married, she still went to church every Sunday. In 1914, Kate and Jeu Gong's first child, Berta, was born. After Berta came a daughter, Martha, and a son, Biscoe.

The Lums soon moved to Rosedale and opened a new store there in order to let their children receive good educations. In the autumn of 1924, Berta and Martha, who were in the third grade and fourth grades respectively, headed off to their first day of school at Rosedale Consolidated School, which was one of the best schools in the Delta.

Both girls were sent home by noon. The new school superintendent told them that the Rosedale Consolidated School Board would not permit Chinese children to enter a school for white students.

This news was like a slap in the face for Kate. She heard that former Mississippi governor Earl Brewer was a lawyer who had helped Chinese clients before. Kate and Jeu Gong decided to ask him to file a lawsuit on their behalf against the school board of trustees, including members L.C. Brown, Greek P. Rice, and Henry McGowen.

Brewer told the court that nine-year-old Martha had been born in Mississippi, and was an outstanding student. She had been banned from an all-white school purely because of racial discrimination, as she was of Chinese descent. This violated the Fourteenth Amendment of the Constitution. In addition, Mississippi State law stipulated that students between the ages of five to eighteen could not be prohibited from entering school. Therefore, Martha's right to go to school was also protected by state law.

The board of trustees offered the following defense. Refusing Martha's right to enter Rosedale Consolidated School was legal under Article 207 of the Mississippi State Constitution, which permitted schools to segregate white students from black students. Since Martha counted as one of the "Mongolian or yellow" race, she could only attend schools for "colored" students.

On 5 November 1924, the circuit court judge William Alcorn dismissed this defense and ordered that Rosedale Consolidated School accept Martha as a student.

The board of trustees, who had powerful forces of racial segregation behind them, did not stop there. On December 15th, they filed an appeal to the Mississippi Supreme Court, with the state attorney-general acting as their head lawyer. At the time, no other Chinese families had joined Kate's lawsuit. Although the Lum family stood alone, they were determined to keep fighting.

169

As the most important case in the state supreme court opened, Elmer Clinton Sharp, who represented the board of trustees, declared that Mississippi State policy had always permitted the existence of white schools dedicated for white children. Martha and other children of Chinese descent should be classified as "Negroes." The State had "created" a system of racial segregation to protect white interests, so there was no need to consider the Federal Constitution.

Brewer pointed out that when the system of segregated schools was created in 1890, only blacks and whites lived in Mississippi. Martha was a resident of the state. No matter what her skin color was, she had the right to an education at public schools in the state. However, the Supreme Court of Mississippi ruled that since Martha was not white, she could not enter Rosedale Consolidated School to attend school with other white students.

The Lum family had lost. Kate decided to send her students to Michigan to attend a non-segregated school. In May 1925, the 11-year old Berta took her 10-year old sister and 6-year old brother onto a train headed north, sitting in the designated "Colored People" car. At least the fact that all non-white students at the school were treated equally brought some small comfort to the sisters' broken hearts.

At this time J.K. Young, a Chinese businessman, extended a helping hand to Kate's family. His ancestors had long ago arrived in the Delta and opened a grocery store in Tunika, a town south of Memphis. He had been closely following the development of the case. After Brewer lost the lawsuit, he volunteered to write a letter to the Supreme Court, acting as a representative of the Lum family, asking for documents from previous trials and for the case to be reopened.

On 21 November 1927, Supreme Court Judge William Taft issued a unanimous ruling from all nine judges. They believed that the crucial question of this case was whether children with Chinese blood born in the United States were denied equal protection by the law if they were only able to attend schools that only accepted brown, yellow, or black students. However, in the end, the ruling supported the policy of racial segregation.

Within a few days, the case ruling was published in major newspapers across the United States. This meant that Chinese people in the Delta had done their utmost to resist the decision but had ultimately lost.

Kate continued to search for a solution to her children's education. At last, she found a school in a town called Elaine, just across the Mississippi River in Arkansas, that was willing to accept her children into a school for white students. Although the school building was quite old and the teacher qualifications low, Kate and her family still left Rosedale, moved near the new school, and opened a small grocery store. Because the Chinese were not allowed to own real estate property back then, the Lum family's toils of the past ten years were reduced to nothing, and they were forced to start over from poverty. The business from the grocery store wasn't enough to make ends meet. Kate would get up early every morning to bake bread to support her family. In her heart, she still held onto a small glimmer of hope.

In 1933, Berta and Martha graduated from high school. Martha majored in education at Arkansas State University. After the start of World War II, the two sisters went to Long Beach, California to work in a munitions factory assembling pieces for bomber planes. Their little brother joined the military in 1940, and was later deployed to Yunnan, China to work in a hospital at an American air base.

Kate Lum and her family never gave up in the long battle for the defense of the constitutional guarantee of equality against racial discrimination. It was not until 1954 that the Supreme Court ruled in Brown vs. Board of Education that the system of racial segregation violated the Constitution.

This ruling also overruled the 1927 ruling against the Lum family based on the legality of segregation. From that point on, the barriers formed by racism could finally be dismantled.

看图写作训练

图片创作： 韩 梅